Buon Appetito!

Jeffy Cote de Luna

DELICACIES

Make Every Meal Extraordinary

Jeffery Cote de Luna

Wine Pairings
Kaitlin Lucarelli, Eataly Chicago

Photography
Jeffery Cote de Luna

Art Direction
Gregory Zychowicz

This book is dedicated to all the students with whom I have had the pleasure of sharing the art and culture of Italy. They have helped me see Italy with fresh eyes on every visit.

First Edition
ISBN: 978-0-578-69993-6

Contents

Foreword *by David Brody*

It's great to have friends with whom you share abiding interests, and Jeffery has been my great "food" friend. Over the years we've exchanged recipes, suggestions on kitchen equipment, and tips on new ingredients. I've also been a guest at his table on numerous occasions. Each was something special to look forward to and, later, remember.

Jeffery doesn't do things by half-measures; he goes all-out. Recently, I've had the extra pleasure of a front row seat as he's tested and re-tested his recipes and sorted through materials for this book. I've received email updates on everything

from *guanciale* –

I started curing a 1.5 pound piece. . . today. . . A week or two in the brine and then into a Umai Dry bag for a few weeks. My fridge is getting pretty full with charcuterie.

to rabbit –

I want to share this recipe for coniglio ripieno in porchetta. *It's seriously the best thing I've made all summer.*

to sausage –

I tried out my new sausage stuffer today. I made five pounds of 'lamb' chorizo and five pounds of finocchiona. *It was pretty much an all day affair. It took about five hours, including cleanup between meats. . .*

His many emails always evinced a high level of enthusiasm and an ever-increasing culinary knowledge.

I've known Jeffery for over thirty-five years. We met in the early 1980s as graduate students in painting at Yale University. He was already quite a skillful artist, possessed a depth of knowledge, and applied himself with real discipline in the studio. As our careers progressed, we both became professors, and I came to know him as a highly dedicated teacher, one who generously shared his wealth of knowledge with his students. Over the years I've also had the pleasure of hosting him as a visiting artist on a number of occasions; first, while I was teaching in Florence in the 1990s; and, in more recent decades, at the University of Washington in Seattle, where I've been teaching since. His lectures were always insightful, beautifully illustrated, and composed with great care.

Jeffery brings all of this experience and craft to this book, making it much more than a collection of fine recipes. He's been a successful teacher and really knows how to break things down into cogent steps so that other people can reproduce his results. And the photographs constitute a riveting body of work in and of themselves. Jeffery has brought all his visual sophistication and high standards to bear. As he writes, "I obsessively photograph. . . most of the meals that I cook." He adds that he takes "a few dozen shots from different angles, moving food and garnishes around the plate like chess pieces." That is, indeed, the painter I've known. Everything's been arranged so that every color, shape, and cast shadow appears in just the right amount, in just the right place to create a stunning composition. He's never shied away from the hard work needed to accomplish wonderful things, whether that's been in the studio, the classroom, the kitchen, or, now, in creating this book. It's a great pleasure to leaf through the pages and enjoy the photographs visually. I'm now looking forward to many a fine meal as I make my way through the recipes themselves and enjoy them gastronomically.

Introduction

Making extraordinary meals is satisfying and requires little more than a love for food and a passion for cooking. Fortunately, extraordinary meals often contain ordinary ingredients. Many of my favorite dishes are examples of *la cucina povera* or peasant cooking. *Zuppa di pesce* (fisherman's stew) is typically made with the small fish that did not sell on the harbor on a given day. Because it is made with several different kinds of fish and shellfish, it becomes a rich and complex delicacy far greater than the sum of its parts. *Coda alla vaccinara* (oxtail stew) is another example of *la cucina povera*. Butchers learned that if they braised this largely unwanted, tough cut of meat and bone over low heat for a long period of time, it could be transformed into a fall-off-the-bone delicacy. Day-old bread has often been used to augment and extend a meal from *ribollita* (a bread, bean, and cabbage soup) to *panzanella* (a bread and tomato salad from Tuscany). In southern Italy, bread crumbs, instead of costlier grated cheese, are often sprinkled over pasta. Bread crumbs are especially delicious sautéed in olive oil with some garlic and sprinkled over *spaghetti con le sarde* (spaghetti with sardines).

For the past twenty-five years I have been fortunate to have had the opportunity to live and teach in Italy for several months a year courtesy of Dominican University, where I teach painting and drawing in a suburb outside Chicago. During my visits to Italy, I have fallen in love not only with Italian cuisine but also with the manner in which the Italians eat well. By that I mean shopping in the local farmers' markets, small butcher shops, and at the fishmongers; buying freshly made bread, cheese, and pasta from artisans who know their customers' names; eating what is in season; cooking with passion and generosity; and enjoying long leisurely meals. These may not take place every evening at my home, but I like to make them a part of my life at least once a week, usually on Sundays. I've truly enjoyed adding "food culture" to Dominican University's study abroad programs in Florence and Rome. In Florence, where I rent a large apartment during the summer, I look forward to making a few "family meals" for my students and colleagues. In Rome, where we all stay in a hotel during the winter interim, I work closely with our travel agent to curate the group dinners to ensure that students are exposed to *la vera cucina romana* or authentic Roman cuisine.

Throughout Italy, Italians begin their meal with an *aperitivo* to open up and whet the appetite. An *aperitivo* might be a simple glass of *prosecco* or an *Aperol spritz* with friends at a nearby bar. The *antipasto* or starter course might include a few slices of cured meat, some fresh *ricotta*, or sautéed mussels, depending on the region. The *primo* or first course is often a small portion of *pasta* or *risotto* with a light sauce. The *secondo* or main course can be fish or meat-based and is accompanied by one or two *contorni* or side dishes. The wine consumed is generally local to the region and part of the same *terroir* as the meal. I usually skip dessert as I have in this book, opting instead for some local cheese and honey. The meal begins to come to an end with a small cup of *espresso* and a *digestivo*, such as a barrel-aged *grappa*, made with the pulp of the grapes used to make the wine that was enjoyed with the meal. If Sunday afternoon meals like this appeal to you, then I think you will enjoy this book. These are the dishes that I find myself making over and over again both for myself and for my friends. *Buon appetito!*

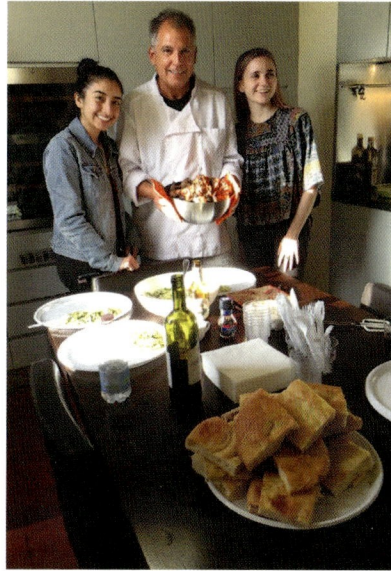

Thoughts on Photographing Food

According to a recent study by the market research firm Marumatchbox, sixty-nine percent of millennials in America photograph their food before eating it. Although far from being a millennial, I obsessively photograph and Instagram most of the meals that I cook and many that I eat in restaurants. I'm not sure when I started this performance of photographing my food and sharing it with the world, as if anyone really cares what I have for lunch on any given day. It contradicts everything that I know and teach my students about being present in the moment. I want my students to see Caravaggio's paintings with their own eyes – not through the LCD screen on their cameras. I want them to walk around and experience Bernini's sculptures in three dimensions from different angles before they compress them into two-dimensional backlit memories. Basically, I want them to *smell the incense before snapping the image.*

So, why can't I hold myself to these same standards when I'm eating in a restaurant? Food is a multi-sensual experience. Smell, taste, mouthfeel, color, texture, composition, temperature, memories – food is all of these, so it's virtually impossible to photograph. Numerous studies have shown that individuals that fully engage with a work of art will remember it far better than those who instead photographed the experience. The same goes for food. Last year I experienced a creative and well-thought out tasting menu at Alinea, Grant Achatz' three-star Michelin restaurant in Chicago. Unfortunately, I was so preoccupied with documenting each plate that six months later I could barely recall what I ate. Unfortunately, you can't eat food first and then photograph it, although some chefs are happy to send their customers professional shots of their dinner; if only they would stop taking pictures and eat the damn meal.

While some chefs have tried to ban photography in their restaurants, stating that it disrupts the meal, others encourage it, knowing that their plates will end up on TripAdvisor and Yelp. I'm not sure that's such a great advantage, however, since those restaurant websites are filled with poorly lit, half eaten meals, shot under incandescent lighting. If you insist, as I apparently do, to photograph your food, there are a few things to keep in mind. You can take excellent photos with your iPhone as long as you have natural daylight. Sit by the window, and wear white to reflect light. Remember that restaurants work hard to get their food out while it's still hot. Shoot quickly and enjoy your meal. That being said, I have eaten few meals described in this book as presented in my photographs. By the time I've taken a few dozen shots from different angles, moving food and garnishes around the plate like chess pieces, the food is stone cold. It then gets thrown back into the frying pan to be reheated and unceremoniously dumped back on my plate, where on occasion, it looks better than the first plate, requiring another round of photos and a return to the stove.

Utensili da Cucina
Kitchen Equipment

I don't own a microwave; I haven't had one for over twenty years. I also don't own a Crock-Pot, Instant Pot, pressure cooker, or rice cooker. No doubt these items can be useful, but I simply don't have the counter space or storage space in my kitchen. Here's what I do have on my countertop: a Dualit toaster (handy for making garlic toast; I don't eat breakfast), a La Pavoni espresso maker (I couldn't live without it), a KitchenAid Professional stand mixer (with pasta rolling and meat grinding attachments), an Anova Precision sous vide cooker inserted into a 12 quart polycarbonate tub, a good quality kitchen scale that converts to grams, and an Italian Berkel meat slicer that takes up approximately 3 square feet of precious real estate. I only use the slicer a half dozen times a year, but it looks so badass that it stays.

Above my range, hangs a large array of stainless steel spoons, spatulas, ladles, skimmers, tongs, graters, kitchen spiders, and conical sieves. For these items I'm partial to the German manufacturer Rösle. My collection of German, Italian, and Japanese knives hang on a long magnet bar above my work table; I like knives. Stored inside the drawers under my counter, are my stand blender, immersion blender, food processor, Smoking Gun, Thermapen, Benriner mandoline, a propane torch, and an assortment of stainless steel bowls, measuring cups, and measuring spoons. My pots, pans, and woks all hang from a ceiling mounted pot rack within arm's reach of my work table.

Nella Dispensa
In the Pantry

I shop like an Italian *nonna*; that is, I shop for fresh fish, meat, and produce on a daily basis. Luckily, I live in Chicago where we have an Eataly, Whole Foods, good butcher shops, and fish mongers. In addition, there are many weekly farmers' markets in the summer and fall. The following items are things that I always have on hand, to make "make every meal extraordinary".

In the cupboard:
Very good extra-virgin olive oil, red and white vinegar, Arborio rice, Afeltra brand pasta (*spaghettoni*, *linguine*, *rigatoni*, and *paccheri*), several cans of Afeltra brand San Marzano tomatoes, Afeltra brand *pomodorini* (cherry tomatoes), finishing salts (including Maldon smoked salt and truffle salt), fennel pollen, *pimentón* de la Vera, saffron, anchovies, capers, *mostarde*, an assortment of Italian honey, and a jar of Planter's peanuts to go with my *Negronis*.

In the fridge:
A six-pack of Peroni beer, grated bottarga, cuttlefish ink, a large plastic bag of *peperoncini*, mixed olives, Mutti brand *doppio concentrato di pomodoro* (double concentrate tomato paste), fresh eggs, *Parmigiano*, *Pecorino*, and a big hunk of *guanciale* (cured pork cheek) that I use for any recipe calling for *pancetta* (Italian bacon). I also cure my own *salumi*, so there's plenty of that in the fridge as well.

In the freezer:
Butter (yes, store your butter in the freezer), SAF instant yeast, homemade beef stock, chicken stock, and fish stock (stored in 2 cup containers), and a couple of bags of frozen peas (to reduce swelling from running injuries).

L'APERITIVO

Italians are devoted to *l'aperitivo*. A drink with friends before dinner at a bar or café is something nearly everyone takes part in, from Milan to Palermo. It's an important part of the Italian meal structure. It could be a cocktail like a *Negroni* or an *Aperol spritz*, or simply a glass of *prosecco* or white wine, or even a glass of vermouth. The word, *aperitivo*, comes from the Latin verb *aperire*, meaning to open. The idea is not only to socialize but to "open the appetite." This is generally done with some small snacks provided without charge by the café. The food can be as simple as a bowl of nuts or chips, to something more substantial, such as *pizzette* (tiny bite-size pizzas), or tiny triangular *tramezzini* (white bread sandwiches with the crusts removed). Some places serve *apericena*, which is a lavish buffet-style meal offered for the price of a cocktail. At these places, you might be spending 12 Euros for your cocktail, but you'll be eating pricey cheeses and cured meats, maybe even a little pasta. If you care about maintaining *la bella figura*, or proper form, *aperitivo* time is generally between 19:00 and 21:00.

Aperol Spritz

This orange concoction is the cocktail that everyone seems to be drinking at *aperitivo* time in Venice. Add some peanuts, or some *cicchetti* (small snacks), and you're good to go until your restaurant opens.

Serves 1
· 2 oz *Prosecco*
· 2 oz Aperol
· Splash of soda

Directions
Pour *prosecco,* Aperol and soda over ice; stir and garnish with an orange slice.

Negroni

The *Negroni* is the perfect *aperitivo*. It's a symmetrically balanced cocktail made with equal parts Campari, sweet vermouth, and dry gin. The Campari contributes a warm spicy bitterness; the vermouth adds sweetness and complexity; and the gin adds piney, citrusy notes. In my opinion, the only foods that go well with a *Negroni* are potato chips and peanuts. Their saltiness complements the flavors of the *Negroni* perfectly and prepares you for your evening meal. In Rome, my absolute favorite place to have a *Negroni* is at Antonini Bar Pasticceria in the Prati district north of the Vatican. This bar, with tables and chairs lining the storefront, caters to the inhabitants of the upscale residential neighborhood. There are no sights to see in this neighborhood; therefore, there are few, if any, tourists. The staff is very friendly, and with every drink they will bring out a tray of small bites.

Serves 1
· 1 1/2 oz Campari
· 1 1/2 oz sweet vermouth
· 1 1/2 oz dry gin

Directions
Pour Campari, gin, and sweet vermouth over ice; stir and garnish with an orange slice.

Negroni Sbagliato

It's almost impossible to screw up a *Negroni*, yet someone once did substituting *Prosecco* in place of gin. It turns out the *Negroni Sbagliato* or messed up *Negroni* is a pleasantly lighter and more refreshing version of the traditional cocktail.

Serves 1
· 1 1/2 oz Campari
· 1 1/2 oz sweet vermouth
· 1 1/2 oz *Prosecco*

Directions
Pour Campari, sweet vermouth, and *prosecco* over ice, stir, and garnish with an orange slice.

Americano

This is the lightest most refreshing version of the trio of Campari cocktails.

Serves 1
· 1 1/2 oz Campari
· 1 1/2 oz sweet vermouth
· 1 1/2 oz soda water

Directions
Pour Campari, sweet vermouth, and soda water over ice; stir and garnish with an orange slice.

ANTIPASTI

Crostone di Pane all'Aglio
Garlic Bread

Ingredients
- Hearty country bread loaf cut into 1/2" thick slices and toasted
- 2 garlic cloves, halved crosswise
- 2 tablespoons olive oil

Directions
Toast the bread in the oven until golden; rub with garlic and brush with olive oil.

Baccalà Mantecato
Whipped Salt Cod

One of the great pleasures of visiting Venice is getting lost in the maze of narrow streets, canals, and alleyways, before stumbling upon a *bàcaro* or wine bar off the beaten track. In Venice your phone's GPS is always in beta mode, so relax and have an *Aperol Spritz* or glass of local wine and order a couple of *cicchetti* – think Spanish tapas. *Baccalà mantecato* seems to be everyone's favorite *cicchetto*, and it is ubiquitous throughout the city. It's made from salt cod whipped with oil until creamy. My favorite places to eat it are at Al Mercà, next to the Rialto Market; La Cantina near the Ca' d'Oro; and the legendary Cantinone già Schiavi in Dorsoduro. The latter makes a garlicky version that I like very much. They also add finely chopped parsley, so the customers can tell the garlic and non-garlic versions apart. Traditional recipes call for extra-virgin olive oil; however, these days most Venetians use sunflower oil, which allows the flavor of the fish to ascend while keeping the dish creamy white. Using a rolling pin to beat the salt cod and oil has also given way to the *planetaria* or stand mixer.

Wine Pairing
Casa Coste Piane Prosecco Valdobiaddene, Veneto

Makes about 20 crostini
· 1 pound salt cod
· 1 quart milk
· 1/2 small onion
· 1 teaspoon whole black peppercorns
· 2 bay leaves
· 6 garlic cloves
· 1/2 teaspoon salt
· 2 tablespoons Italian parsley, finely minced
· 3/4 cup sunflower oil, or 1/2 cup sunflower oil and 1/4 cup extra-virgin olive oil
· 1-2 baguettes cut into 1/2" diagonal slices

Directions
Soak the salt cod in cold water in the refrigerator for 2 days, changing water twice a day.

Once the cod has lost its saltiness, place in a saucepan and cover with milk. Add onion, peppercorns, bay leaves, and 3 smashed garlic cloves. Simmer for 20-25 minutes. Be careful not to let the milk boil.

Remove cod from milk and place in the bowl of a stand mixer with 2 tablespoons reserved cooking milk. Mix on medium speed with a beater attachment until cod has broken apart. Add three cloves of fresh garlic crushed with a garlic press, 2 tablespoons minced parsley, and 1/2 teaspoon salt (if needed). Beat for a minute to mix, add sunflower oil in a slow steady stream. Stop to scrape down sides of bowl from time to time and continue to beat until creamy.

Check for salt and serve on good quality baguette slices.

Frittata Cipolla e Salsiccia
Omelet with Onion and Sausage

Savory *frittate* are easy to make and are served for lunch at many cafes and bars in Italy. They are delicious with a green salad and few slices of hearty bread. What isn't eaten at lunch is often cut into bite-sized snacks that are given away in the evening during *l'aperitivo*. My *frittata* is made with onions, Italian sausage, and cheese, but you can use any combination of vegetables, greens, meats, and cheeses that you wish. If you're new to making *frittate*, I recommend that you keep the ratio of eggs to filling close to the recipe below.

Wine Pairing
Serafini & Vidotto Rosé Bollicine, Veneto

Serves 4-6
· 1 tablespoon extra-virgin olive oil
· 1 medium onion, sliced thin
· Salt, to taste
· Black pepper, freshly ground to taste
· 1 teaspoon fennel seeds
· 1/2 pound hot Italian sausage (2 links)
· 6 large eggs, preferably cage free & organic
· 1/4 cup Italian parsley, coarsely chopped
· 1/2 cup *Parmigiano Reggiano*, freshly grated
· 4 ounces fresh *mozzarella*, sliced and cut into 2" pieces

Directions
Preheat oven to broil.

In a 10" nonstick frying pan heat olive oil over medium heat. Add onions, salt, pepper, fennel seeds and sauté until onions are soft. Remove sausages from their casings and crumble on top of the onions. Continue to break up the sausages with a wooden spoon and cook until browned.

In a medium-sized bowl, season eggs with a pinch of salt and pepper and whisk to blend. Mix in parsley and ¼ cup *Parmigiano*.

Add eggs to the frying pan and quickly stir with the onion and sausage. Let set for about 3 minutes over medium heat. Insert *mozzarella* into the omelet and sprinkle remaining 1/4 cup *Parmigiano* on top. Continue cooking until eggs are almost firm. At this point, place frying pan on the top shelf under the broiler for 3-4 minutes until cheeses have melted and browned.

Remove pan from the oven (remember to use a pot holder or oven mitt). Loosen the omelet on the sides and bottom with a silicone spatula and slide onto a large plate. Allow to cool for 10 minutes before slicing.

Impepata di Cozze
Peppered Mussels

Europeans love mussels, and these shellfish can be found everywhere – from Ireland, where they are prepared with cream, to Belgium, where they are cooked in beer, to Southern France, where tomatoes and onions are added. The Italian manner of preparing them with black pepper is the simplest, lightest, and, in my opinion, the best. *Impepata di cozze* evokes memories of many summer lunches at the seaside Ristorante Sa Playa in Viareggio.

Wine Pairing

Fattoria Sardi Rosato, Toscana

Serves 2-4

· 2 pounds mussels
· 5 tablespoons extra-virgin olive oil
· 2 garlic cloves, smashed
· 1/4 cup dry white wine
· Salt, to taste
· Black pepper, freshly ground to taste
· 1 tablespoon Italian parsley, finely minced

Directions

Wash and debeard the mussels, set aside.

Heat olive oil and garlic in a large Dutch oven over medium heat until fragrant. Add mussels, white wine, and a pinch of salt; cover and cook 4-5 minutes over medium-high heat. Shake the pot back and forth a few times. After a few minutes check on mussels and give them a couple of stirs. Add freshly ground pepper (don't be shy; this should be a peppery dish). Once mussels have opened, serve in the same pot or pour into a serving platter. Sprinkle with chopped parsley and drizzle a little more olive oil.

Serve with the best, crunchiest baguette you can find. In Chicago that means a baguette from Eataly or Publican Quality Bread.

Insalata di Mare
Seafood Salad

I love seafood salads but generally avoid ordering them in Italy, as they are often too acidic. At home, I can control the ratio of olive oil to lemon juice, as well as the mixture and proportions of seafood. My recipe for *insalata di mare* calls for the addition of a little rendered *guanciale* and *peperoncino*. Feel free to leave either or both out if you wish. You can also add or substitute other shellfish, such as clams and scallops. It's best served at room temperature. This is beach food through and through.

Wine Pairing

Colli di Lapio di Romano Clelia Fiano d'Avellino, Campania

Serves 4-6

· 1 pound *calamari*, 1/2 tubes and 1/2 tentacles
· 1 pound baby octopus
· 1/2 pound medium shrimp
· 1 pound mussels (about 3 dozen)
· 1 teaspoon white wine vinegar
· 1/4 cup dry white wine
· 1 medium yellow wax potato
· 1/4 cup + 1 tablespoon extra-virgin olive oil
· 2 teaspoons fresh lemon juice
· Salt, to taste
· 1/4 teaspoon white pepper, freshly ground
· *Peperoncino*, to taste
· 1 tablespoon Italian parsley, finely minced
· 2 garlic cloves, smashed
· 18 black *Gaeta* or *Niçoise* olives, un-pitted
· 2 oz thinly sliced *guanciale*, cut into lardons

Directions

Cut *calamari* into 1/4" rings. Leave tentacles intact. Remove the head of the octopus below the eyes; discard eyes and cut head into 1/4" rings. Separate the eight tentacles. Shell and devein shrimp. Scrub and debeard mussels. Peel potato and cut into 1/2" cubes; place in cold water so that it doesn't discolor.

Sauté mussels in a sauce pan over medium-high heat with 1/4 cup dry white wine. Remove mussels and reserve. Add 1 quart water and cook potatoes in the saucepan over medium-low heat for about 8 minutes until tender. Remove with a slotted spoon and set aside. Add a tablespoon of salt to the water and cook shrimp over medium-low heat for 3 minutes until pink. Remove shrimp and set aside. Add *calamari* and cook over medium-low for 5 minutes. Remove and set aside. Pour out all but a 1/4 cup of cooking liquid, add octopus and vinegar, simmer over very low heat for 45 minutes. Add more water if needed. Be careful not to tear the purple skin. Let octopus cool down in its own liquid. While octopus is cooking, remove mussels from their shells.

Once octopus has cooled, place into a large bowl with the mussels, shrimp, *calamari* and potatoes. In a small bowl, whisk 1/4 cup of olive oil with 2 teaspoons freshly squeezed lemon juice and add to seafood and potato mixture. Add salt, white pepper, black olives and garlic, and let marinate on the counter for one hour. Give it a gentle stir with a silicon spatula every so often.

While the salad is marinating, sauté the *guanciale* in a tablespoon of olive oil with the *peperoncino* over low heat until the fat is rendered and the *guanciale* is crisp (about 10 minutes). Remove *guanciale* from pan and set aside.

When ready to serve, remove garlic, check seasonings, add *guanciale* and freshly minced parsley. Don't forget to remind your guests that the olives are un-pitted.

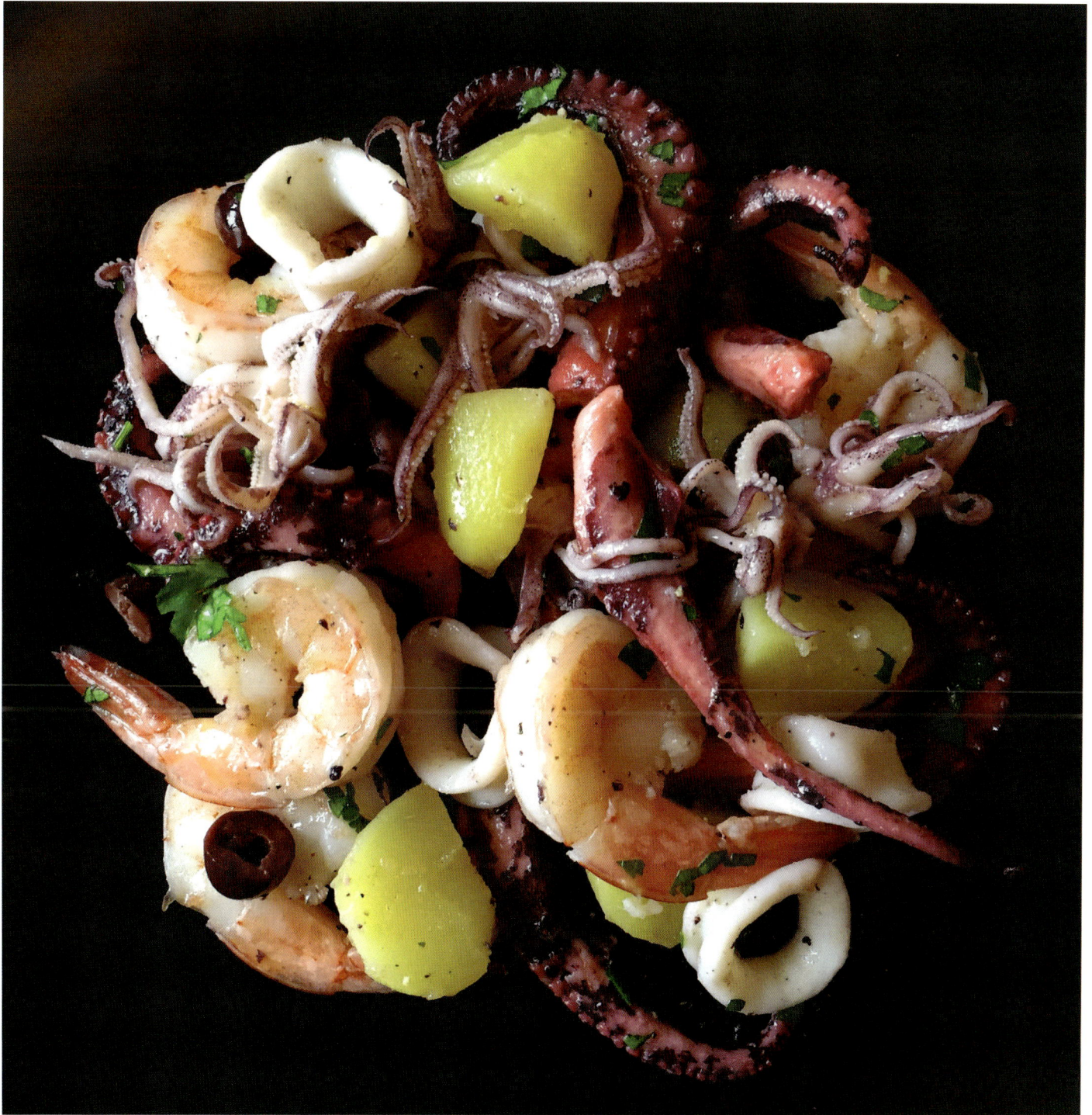

Insalta di Salmone Affumicato
Smoked Salmon Salad

Several years ago, I discovered the Enoteca Cul de Sac in the heart of Rome near the Piazza Navona. My hotel happened to be nearby, and I would walk past it every day. I noticed that it was very busy at lunchtime with mostly locals waiting in line to get in. Cul de Sac is a small, bustling wine bar/restaurant with wooden booths inside and a few tables outside on the Piazza di Pasquino. The ambience is decidedly authentic. Its menu offers traditional Roman cuisine along with a large variety of *taglieri* or wooden boards topped with homemade *patés*, cured meats, cheeses, and smoked fish. It also has an extensive wine list with over 1,500 wines. I'm a pushover for cured and smoked fish, and their *misto mare affumicato* (mixed smoked seafood) never disappoints. On my last visit, it featured salmon, swordfish, and herring, all delicately cured and lightly smoked, served over arugula and sliced red onions – the perfect lunch.

Wine Pairing

Alberico Appia Antica Bianco, Lazio

Ingredients

· 2 pounds salmon fillet (skin on, pinbones removed, and cut into two rectangular pieces)
· 1/2 cup raw sugar
· 1 cup light brown sugar
· 3/4 cup kosher salt
· 1/4 cup *Pastis* (an anise flavored liqueur)
· 1 fennel bulb thinly sliced, fronds reserved
· 1/2 cup toasted fennel seeds
· 2 tablespoons toasted white peppercorns, crushed
· Fennel pollen

Directions

Mix salt and sugars in a small bowl. Slice fennel thinly on a mandoline. (Use the finger guard and wear cut resistant gloves; these things are very sharp). I am partial to the Japanese Benriner. Toast fennel seeds and white peppercorns separately, tossing over medium heat. Don't leave unattended; they can burn quickly.

Place half the salt/sugar mixture in a large freezer bag and place salmon pieces side by side over the salt, skin side down. Pour *Pastis* over the salmon and cover with remaining salt/sugar mixture. Lay fennel slices on top of the salmon, followed by fennel seeds and crushed white peppercorns.

Close bag, eliminating as much air as possible, and place in a 9"x13" sheet pan. Cover with another 9"x13" sheet pan and weigh it down with a couple of bricks or heavy cans and refrigerate for 48 hours. Pressing the fish will speed up the water loss. Every twelve hours or so, flip over the bag containing the fish.

Fish should be firm after 48 hours. Remove and wash thoroughly to remove salt/sugar mixture and spices. Dry with paper towels and place in the refrigerator uncovered for another 12-24 hours in a 9" x 13" sheet pan with a rack. This will give the salmon a sticky pellicle that will better absorb the smoke. I use the Breville PolyScience Smoking Gun to smoke my fish. Place fish into a new large freezer bag, slide smoking tube into the bag, close bag, follow smoking gun directions.

Once the fish has cured and has been smoked, slice very thinly with a sharp slicing knife and serve over arugula, thinly sliced fresh fennel, and sliced red onion. To take the bite out of the red onion, soak for an hour in ice water with a tablespoon of white wine vinegar. Drizzle salad with olive oil, sprinkle with fennel pollen, and garnish with fennel fronds. It makes for a delicious antipasto. Smoked salmon is also delicious on a pizza with fresh *burrata* and *rucola*.

Panzanella
Bread and Tomato Salad

This bread and summer vegetable salad is a Tuscan classic with deep roots in *la cucina povera* or peasant cooking. Actually, there's no cooking involved with this dish, making it an excellent choice for a hot summer day. I first had it at the colorful and atmospheric Osteria Belle Donne in Florence many years ago. My colleagues and I used to go there with our students. It was near our hotel and was relatively inexpensive. There was always a cornucopia of fresh vegetables on top of the counter along with a large bowl filled with refreshing *insalata di panzanella*. Think of it as Spanish *gazpacho*, except with more bread than tomatoes. Use the heartiest country style bread you can find. Some recipes call for bread and tomatoes only. Others include tuna. I prefer this crunchier version with cucumbers and red onions. The *panzanella* shown here was made with two-day old bread from a beautiful artisanal country *boule* made by my friend, chef Nancy Carey, who uses locally sourced grains milled at Janie's Farm, 80 miles south of Chicago.

Wine Pairing
La Spinetta Il Rose di Casanova

Serves 4-6
· 1 pound day old Tuscan-style country bread
· 1/2 red onion
· 1 medium hothouse English cucumber
· 2 large heirloom tomatoes
· 3 tablespoons white wine vinegar
· Fresh basil (12-15 large leaves)
· 6 tablespoons extra-virgin olive oil
· Salt, to taste
· Black pepper, freshly ground to taste

Directions
Remove bread crusts; tear bread into 1" pieces; add to a large bowl with 1 tablespoon of water and 1 tablespoon of white wine vinegar.

Peel and cut onion into 1/4" slices. Soak in ice water with 1 tablespoon of white wine vinegar for one hour. Peel and cut cucumber into 1" cubes and add to the bowl with the bread.

Core and cut tomatoes into 1" pieces; remove seeds and add to the bowl. Drain onions; snap the longer pieces in half and add to the bowl. Tear basil leaves with your hands and add to the salad.

Add 6 tablespoons olive oil, remaining tablespoon of vinegar, salt, and freshly ground pepper to taste. Adjust olive oil and vinegar ratio to taste.

Patè di Fegatini Toscani
Chicken Liver Paté, Tuscan Style

I think *taglieri* or wooden boards topped with an assortment of cured meats, sausages and cheeses make for a great *antipasto*. Many restaurants in Italy serve it in several sizes meant for sharing among friends and family. When I'm on my own I often order a smaller board for my main course with a bottle of local red wine. A convivial restaurant in Florence offering *taglieri* is La Beppa Fioraia near the Piazzale Michelangelo.

For several years, I've been curing my own *salumi*, using the Umai Dry Charcuterie and Sausage Kits. Their products allow you to safely cure meats and sausages in the refrigerator. I encourage you to check them out online. You can also easily assemble your own *tagliere* using store bought *salumi*. A well-rounded *tagliere* should include *coppa* (cured pork neck muscle) *lonza stagionato* (cured pork loin), *lardo* (cured pork back fat), *bresaola* (cured beef), local *salami* including *finocchiona, soppressata, mortadella,* and regional *prosciutto*. In Tuscany, *patè di fegatini di pollo* (chicken liver paté) is often included on a *tagliere*. Many restaurants in Florence also serve *fegatini* as a stand-alone *antipasto*. Unfortunately, it can be hit or miss. The recipe below is a slow cooked explosion of sweet, sour, and salty flavors. Make sure you use good quality *vin santo* and homemade chicken broth. Cook everything low and slow. You don't want to rush this dish.

Wine Pairing
Frescobaldi Castello di Pomino Chardonnay Benefizio, Toscana

Makes about 20 crostini
· 1 pound chicken livers, rinsed and roughly chopped
· 4 tablespoons extra-virgin olive oil
· 2 tablespoons unsalted butter
· 1 medium red onion, finely chopped
· 4 large sage leaves
· 1 sprig rosemary, finely chopped
· 2 tablespoons capers + 2 tablespoons caper vinegar
· 1 cup *vin santo*
· 2 cups homemade chicken broth, warmed over the stove
· 2 tablespoons anchovy paste
· 2 tablespoon balsamic vinegar
· 1/2 teaspoon salt
· 1/2 teaspoon black pepper, freshly ground

Directions
In a colander rinse the chicken livers under cold running water and roughly chop. Finely chop onion.

Heat olive oil and 1 tablespoon of butter in a 12" frying pan over low heat and sauté onions until they are translucent. Add chicken livers, sage leaves, rosemary, capers, and caper vinegar to the onions and cook over medium-low heat for 10 minutes, until livers are grey. Add *vin santo* and cook over medium heat until alcohol evaporates. Add salt, black pepper, and anchovy paste. Begin adding warm chicken broth, ½ cup at a time, and simmer uncovered over medium-low heat until the broth almost evaporates; continue adding broth ½ cup at a time. The sauce should be light and creamy.

When done, mix in remaining butter and balsamic vinegar. Let cool slightly and transfer to kitchen processor. Pulse a few times to mix; you want a slightly course texture.

Serve warm on toasted slices of a good baguette; garnish with a few capers.

Sauté di Calamari
Sautéed Squid

One of my most memorable summer meals was in a public park a few kilometers west of Trieste in northeast Italy. I was returning to the city by bus after a day on the beach in Grado. As my bus passed a park filled with families enjoying grilled food, I decided to get off and check it out. It turned out to be a socialist-sponsored picnic featuring grilled *calamari*, *ćevapčići* (uncased sausages made from lamb, pork and beef), and inexpensive wine. The experience was delicious and fun!

Wine Pairing

Le Vigne di Zamo Ribolla Gialla,
Friuli Venezia-Giulia

Serves 2-4

· 1 pound *calamari*, 1/2 tubes
  and 1/2 tentacles
· 3 tablespoons extra-virgin olive oil
· 1/4 teaspoon salt
· *Peperoncino*, to taste
· 2-3 garlic cloves, thinly sliced
· 1/4 cup Italian parsley leaves, stems removed

Directions

Rinse and dry *calamari* well with paper towels. With a very sharp knife, score the *calamari* tubes on both sides with 3-4 diagonal cuts; be careful not to cut too deep. Mix the *calamari*, olive oil, salt, *peperoncino*, garlic, and half the parsley in a bowl.

Heat a carbon steel wok to high until smoking, add *calamari* mix and stir with a spatula. Push *calamari* up on the sides of the wok as the liquid is released. Every once in a while, stir *calamari* into the liquid and push back up on the sides of the wok. Once the liquid has evaporated, stir *calamari* and continue to brown for a few more minutes. Overall cooking time is about 8-10 minutes.

Serve with the remaining parsley leaves.

Soppressata di Polpo
Octopus Salami

I first saw *soppressata di polpo* on the menu at a small restaurant in Genova. It was listed as an appetizer and it turned out to be delicious. Octopus meat is full of collagen which, when cooked, turns into gelatin. It is the octopus' own gelatin that holds the cylindrical shape of this unique salami. I saw another version of this dish at the Ristorante La Battigia in Bari, where, they tightly wrap whole cooked octopuses in plastic wrap and refrigerate them until thinly slicing them with a meat slicer.

Wine Pairing

Bisson Bianchetta Genevese "U Pastine," Liguria

Serves 2-4

· 1 whole fresh octopus (3 pounds)
· 4-5 fennel stalks (reserve bulb and fronds)
· 1 medium carrot
· 2 red onions
· 12 cloves garlic, smashed
· 3 sprigs fresh thyme
· 3 sprigs fresh rosemary
· 6 sprigs fresh parsley
· 3 bay leaves
· 2 teaspoons black peppercorns
· 2 teaspoons juniper berries, smashed
· 1/2 cup red wine vinegar
· 4 tablespoons kosher salt

Directions

Wash the octopus under cold water; remove eyes and beak. Roughly chop the fennel stalks and carrot. Peel and quarter the onions.

Place the vegetables, herbs, peppercorns, juniper berries, vinegar, and salt in a 12 quart stock pot with 9 quarts of water and bring to a boil.

Fill another large pot with water and bring to a boil. Holding the head of the octopus with tongs, dip the octopus into the water 6-7 times until the tentacles curl up. This step will insure a more attractive presentation and will protect the purple skin. Once the tentacles have curled, place the octopus in the seasoned water and simmer for 1 hour until tender.

While the octopus cooks, cut off the upper third of a plastic quart water bottle and cut several small holes in the bottom; place plastic bottle in small bowl.

When the octopus is cooked, remove from water and let cool. Once the octopus is cool enough to handle, cut off the head and separate the tentacles. Carefully place the tentacles into the plastic bottle with the suction cups facing outward. Insert another bottle with a slightly smaller diameter, and press down on the octopus. Some of the juice will seep through the holes at the bottom of the bottle. At this point, make 3 vertical cuts on the side of the plastic bottle down to the level of the octopus. Fold the plastic flaps over the octopus, wrap tightly in plastic wrap and refrigerate overnight. Place some weight on top of the octopus or raise it so that it presses against the shelf above it.

Serve with a light *vinaigrette*, orange slices, arugula and thinly sliced fennel; garnish with fennel fronds.

PRIMI—PASTA

Dried Pasta

Art students learn that *form follows function* and that *the whole is greater than the sum of its parts*. When it comes to pasta, nothing is truer than these two phrases. Shape and texture matter. Pasta is available in a wide variety of shapes, lengths, and textures because they are meant to be married to a wide variety of sauces, from delicate and silky to rich and hearty.

The best dried pastas are made in the town of Gragnano, 30 kilometers southeast of Naples. Lying between Mount Vesuvius and the Tyrrhenian Sea, Gragnano has the perfect temperature, wind, and humidity for drying pasta. My favorite artisanal pasta is made by Afeltra. They, like most of the other pasta companies in Gragnano, use high protein durum wheat known as *grano duro*. When milled, it's called *semolino* or semolina in English. They also use bronze extrusion plates that roughens up the surface of the pasta as it's being extruded. This makes the pasta more porous, resulting in more starch being released into the cooking water and more water being absorbed into the pasta. Starchy pasta water is gold when finishing pasta with the sauce, as it helps bind the sauce to the pasta.

I recently bought a large 12 quart stock pot, and it has become my favorite pot for cooking pasta. The diameter is large enough so that long pasta, such as *spaghetti*, can be submerged all at once on its side, and larger quantities of pasta can be cooked without bringing the temperature of the water down. For most of the recipes in this book, 4 quarts of water are fine. To that, I add 1 heaping tablespoon of kosher salt (I don't measure). Salt is important as it flavors the pasta, although you may want to cut back on the salt for seafood sauces that already contain a lot of salt.

Always, always, always finish cooking the pasta with the sauce. Undercook your pasta in salted water, transfer it to the sauce using a pasta fork or a kitchen spider, and finish cooking the pasta in the sauce. Make sure to add some of the pasta water to help bind the two ingredients; starch is glue. Pasta and sauce should be thought of as one entity. Remember, *the whole is greater than the sum of its parts*.

In general, Italians like their pasta served on a plate, not in a bowl. They also like their pasta hot; that's why they twirl long pasta into a mound. And, because they like it hot, they don't wait until everyone else is served. Once its placed in front of you – begin eating.

Most of the pasta recipes in this book call for 8 ounces of pasta for 2-4 individuals. While a 2 ounce portion is small, remember that pasta is just one course in the typical Italian meal structure.

Fresh Pasta

I have to be honest; I don't make a lot of fresh pasta. It's easy to find in Italy and there's an Eataly in Chicago that makes it fresh every day. Even Whole Foods now sells a decent selection of fresh pasta. Here are a few pastas that I do make by hand and one that I make with the pasta attachment for my KitchenAid mixer.

As with pizza dough, it is more precise to weigh out the ingredients rather than using measuring cups and spoons. I prefer to use the metric system when making pasta and weigh out all the ingredients in a large bowl. You will need a kitchen scale that converts to grams. Set the bowl on the scale, reset the scale to zero, and slowly add the ingredients by weight. If you plan to make hand-made pasta, it's a good idea to watch a few how-to videos on YouTube.

Orecchiette

335 grams semolina flour

177 grams (177 ml) warm water

6 grams (1 teaspoon) kosher salt

Place semolina flour in a bowl, make a well, and slowly add salted water. Mix with a fork until dough comes together. Remove dough to a wooden cutting board and knead for 10 minutes, until dough is smooth and stiff. Cover dough with plastic wrap and let rest for 30 minutes. Kneading the dough develops the gluten, which makes the dough firmer and helps the pasta hold its shape. Letting the dough rest relaxes the gluten, making the pasta easier to work with.

Once the dough has rested, cut it into small pieces that can be rolled out with your hands into 1/2' thick ropes, approximately 20" long. Use an ordinary knife to cut and drag a 1/2" piece of dough from the end of the rope toward you. Hold the knife at a 45-degree angle to the cutting board, press and roll dough toward you. Open up each piece of dough with your fingers in the opposite direction to form a bowl shape, and transfer to a sheet pan sprinkled with semolina flour. Repeat with remaining dough. Allow pasta to dry at room temperature for 1 hour.

Fresh Pasta

Cavatelli

335 grams semolina flour

177 grams (177 ml) warm water

6 grams (1 teaspoon) kosher salt

Mix dough and allow to relax as with the *orecchiette* recipe. Once the dough has rested, cut it into small pieces that can be rolled out with your hands into 1/2" thick ropes, approximately 20" long. Use an ordinary knife to cut the rope into 1/2" pieces. Using the tips of your index and middle fingers, press each piece and pull the dough toward you so it lengthens slightly and forms a curl in the middle. Transfer to a sheet pan sprinkled with semolina flour. Repeat with remaining dough. Allow pasta to dry at room temperature for 1 hour.

Trofie

335 grams semolina flour

177 grams (177 ml) warm water

6 grams (1 teaspoon) kosher salt

Mix dough and allow to relax as with the *orecchiette* recipe. Once the dough has rested, cut it into small pieces that can be rolled out with your hands into 1/2" thick ropes, approximately 20" long. Use an ordinary knife to cut the rope diagonally into 1/4" pieces.

Roll the small pieces of dough between the palms of your hands to make 1 1/2" strands that are thinner at the ends and plumper in the center. Next, position a dough scraper at a 45 degree angle to the pasta strands and pull dough gently across the cutting board into a spiral. Transfer to a sheet pan sprinkled with semolina flour. Repeat with remaining dough. Allow pasta to dry at room temperature for 1 hour.

Malloreddus

335 grams semolina flour

177 grams (177 ml) warm water

6 grams (1 teaspoon) kosher salt

Pinch of saffron

Use your fingers to grind the saffron into the warm water and let it sit for 30 minutes to bloom. Mix dough and allow to relax as with the *cavatelli* recipe. Once the dough has rested, cut it into small pieces that can be rolled out with your hands into ½ thick ropes, approximately 20" long. Use an ordinary knife to cut the rope into 1/2" pieces. Using the tips of your index and middle fingers, press each piece and pull the dough on a ridged *gnocchi* board. This will give the *cavatelli* ridges which will create more crevasses to absorb hearty sauces. Transfer to a sheet pan sprinkled with semolina flour. Repeat with remaining dough. Allow pasta to dry at room temperature for 1 hour.

Basic Egg Yolk Dough

250 grams *tipo* 00 flour

4 large egg yolks

1 large whole egg

3 grams (1/2 teaspoon) kosher salt

Place the flour in a large bowl, make a well, add the eggs and salt. Using a fork, beat the eggs and begin to slowly incorporate the eggs and flour until a dough forms. Transfer dough to a lightly floured cutting board and knead dough with the palms of your hands for 10 minutes, until dough is silky and smooth. Knead in a little additional flour if dough is too sticky. Flatten dough into a small flat rectangle, wrap in plastic wrap, and let rest for 30 minutes before using.

When you are ready to roll out your dough, you can do it old school with a rolling pin, or with a pasta roller. I use the pasta roller attachment available for my KitchenAid mixer. Feed the dough through the widest setting on low speed, dust dough with a little flour, fold in half lengthwise, and repeat. Set the roller to the next narrowest setting; feed dough through the roller, dust with flour, and trim dough on both long sides to create an evenly wide sheet. Keep decreasing the thickness of the settings until you have the thickness you want making sure to always run the pasta through each setting twice. For the following pastas you will want your pasta to be about 1/8" thick, so use settings 2 or 3.

Pappardelle

hand cut pasta into 1" inch ribbons, approximately 5-6" long

Fettucine or tagliatelle

hand cut pasta into 1/2" strips, approximately 10" long

Tagliarini

hand cut in 1/8" strips, approximately 10" long

Bìgoli in Salsa

Bìgoli in Onion and Anchovy Sauce

The Venetians are fond of adding vinegar to many of their dishes. Traditionally, vinegar was used by fishermen to preserve their catch. For me, vinegar has been an acquired taste that I have grown to love. Vinegar counters the oiliness of some dishes, such as braised lamb, while complementing the sweetness of other dishes, such *Sardèle in Saór* (sardines marinated in onions and white wine vinegar). On a recent visit to Venice to see the *Biennale Arte*, I ordered a delicious *Guazzetto alla Chioggiotta* (Venetian fish stew enhanced with vinegar), at the highly esteemed Osteria Alle Testiere near the Campo Santa Maria Formosa. On that same trip, I also ordered and tried for the first time *bìgoli in salsa* at Alla Vedova, the famous hundred year-old *osteria* tucked away on Ramo Ca' d'Oro off the busy Strada Nova. *Bìgoli in salsa* is a simple dish with roots in the *cucina povera*. It's made with whole-wheat long pasta served with a sauce made with sautéed onions and anchovies.

Wine Pairing

Venica Sauvignon Blanc,
Friuli Venezia-Giulia

Serves 2-4

· 2 tablespoons extra-virgin olive oil
· 1/4 cup panko bread crumbs
· 1 large yellow onion, thinly sliced
· Salt, to taste
· 2 tablespoons dry white wine
· 16 anchovies in olive oil, drained
· 2 tablespoons white-wine vinegar
· White pepper, freshly ground to taste
· 8 oz whole-wheat *bigoli* pasta
  (or whole-wheat *spaghetti*)
· 2 tablespoons Italian parsley,
  finely chopped

Directions

In a small frying pan, heat 1 tablespoon of olive oil over medium heat. Add bread crumbs and sauté until brown; set aside.

Bring 4 quarts of salted water to a boil in a large pot.

In a 10" frying pan, add 1 tablespoon of olive oil, onions, a pinch of salt and sauté over medium-low heat for 15 minutes stirring often. Lower heat to low and continue cooking onions another 15 minutes until very soft; they should be almost jam-like. Add wine and anchovies. Mash anchovies with a wooden spoon until they disintegrate. Cook an additional 15 minutes over low heat. Add white-wine vinegar, freshly ground white pepper, and another pinch of salt; lower heat to simmer.

Add pasta to the boiling water and cook just shy of *al dente*. Using tongs or a pasta fork, transfer pasta from the pot directly into the frying pan; stir to coat.

Serve pasta on warm plates; garnish each portion with 1/2 tablespoon parsley and ½ tablespoon toasted bread crumbs.

Bucatini all'Amatriciana
Bucatini with Cured Pork Cheek and Tomatoes

This is a classic Roman dish said to have originated from the town of Amatrice, about 100 miles northeast of Rome. Its base is *pasta alla gricia* but with the addition of tomatoes. It was first introduced in Italy in the late 18th century. Like *gricia*, it's an earthy and assertive dish. It's also full of umami flavor from the tomatoes and cheese. In Rome this dish is usually served with thick *bucatini*, while in Amatrice it's served over *spaghetti*. I find *bucatini* a little unwieldy to twirl on my fork, so I usually use the thicker *spaghettoni*.

On August 24, 2016, a massive 6.2 magnitude earthquake devasted the town of Amatrice during the week when it was celebrating the festival or *sagra degli spaghetti all'amatriciana*. Many people lost their lives, and most of the city center was destroyed. Immediately afterward, restaurants all over Italy and the United States began serving spaghetti *all'amatriciana* with a percentage of the proceeds going to relief efforts in Amatrice.

Wine Pairing
Corte dei Papi Cesanese del Piglio
"Colle Ticchio," Lazio

Serves 2-4
· 8 oz *bucatini* (*spaghetti, spaghettoni,* and *rigatoni* are also often used)
· 1 tablespoon extra-virgin olive oil
· 4 oz *guanciale*, cut into 1/4 thick lardons
· *Peperoncino*, to taste
· 2 garlic cloves, thinly sliced
· 1 small red onion, cut in half lengthwise and sliced thinly
· 1/4 cup dry white wine
· 1 bay leaf
· 1/2 teaspoon black pepper, freshly ground
· 14 oz can of whole San Marzano tomatoes, cut tomatoes into strips (save juice for another use)
· Salt, to taste
· 1/2 cup *Pecorino Romano*, freshly grated

Directions
Bring 4 quarts of salted water to boil in a large pot.

In a 12" frying pan, heat olive oil and *guanciale* over medium-low heat and cook until the *guanciale* has rendered its fat and has become crispy. Be patient; avoid the temptation to turn up the heat. Remove half the *guanciale* and set aside. Use these strips to top the pasta when you plate it. Drain about half of the oil.

Add garlic and *peperoncino* and sauté over low heat for about 30 seconds until fragrant. Do not let it brown. Add onions and wine; cook over medium-low heat until wine has evaporated and onions are soft and translucent about 5-10 minutes. Add bay leaf, tomatoes, black pepper, and a pinch of salt and simmer on low for 20-30 minutes. Turn off the heat when done.

Add pasta to the boiling water and cook until just shy of *al dente*. Using tongs or a pasta fork, transfer pasta from the pot directly into the frying pan. Add 2 oz of pasta water to the sauce. Cook 2-3 minutes over medium-high heat, tossing the pasta or shaking the pan while whisking the pasta with tongs. Keep things moving to create a velvety emulsified sauce. If the emulsion breaks down, add a little more pasta water and keep tossing until the emulsion reappears.

Remove from heat, stir in *Pecorino Romano*, and plate, dividing the crispy *guanciale* to place on top of each portion. Serve with additional cheese on the side.

Cacio e Pepe
Pasta with Cheese and Black Pepper

This was always an elusive dish for me. It seemed that no matter how I cooked it, the *Pecorino Romano* would always coagulate. Then, several years ago on a cold New Year's Day in Rome with my friends Emilia Gryc and Davide Ardia, I asked our server at the now closed Ristorante Paris if I could watch how they made their *cacio e pepe*. I was welcomed into the kitchen by the cooks and was generously shown step by step how they made it. This is my adaptation of their recipe.

Wine Pairing
Lungarotti Montefalco Rosso, Umbria

Serves 2-4
· 8 oz *spaghetti* or *rigatoni*
· 1 teaspoon black peppercorns, crushed (you really want them coarse for this dish, try crushing them with a cast iron frying pan on your cutting board).
· 1 cup *Parmigiano Reggiano*, finely grated
· 1/2 cup *Pecorino Romano*, finely grated
· 4 tablespoons unsalted butter
· 3/4 cup pasta water

Directions
Bring 4 quarts of salted water to boil in a large pot; add pasta and cook *al dente*.

In a 10" frying pan, melt 2 tablespoons of butter over medium heat; add crushed black peppercorns and toast one minute. One minute before the pasta is ready, ladle 3/4 cups of starchy pasta water into the frying pan. Add pasta and remaining butter.

Add *Parmigiano Reggiano* over low heat and mix well until melted. Remove from heat and stir in Pecorino Romano until melted and twirl onto warm plates.

Linguine alle Vongole
Linguini with Clams

I love Sunday mornings in Florence. The city is calm and the streets oddly empty. This is the time to visit Ghiberti's *Gates of Paradise* at the Baptistery or the artisan market in the Piazza Santo Spirito. As noon approaches, you begin to smell and hear the sounds of lunch being prepared throughout the city. *Pranzo della Domenica*, or Sunday lunch, is my favorite meal of the week. I like to make it the longest meal of the week. In Florence, I usually start with a *Negroni* along the river at the Chiosco Il Tempio. From there, I walk a few blocks to the Chalet Bellariva, also situated on the river. Both of these spots lie east of the city center and the *viale* or boulevards that follow the outline of the ancient city walls. Few if any tourists go there. The Chalet Bellariva has a large outdoor seating area that is filled with large boisterous Italian families on any given Sunday. I have enjoyed going there for years. I'll often begin with an assortment of thinly sliced cured fish over a bed of arugula as my antipasto, followed by a velvety plate of *linguine alle vongole* as my primo, and grilled fish or octopus as my secondo or main course. Then on to a coffee (I'm not much of a dessert guy) and a glass or two of aged *grappa*. Three hours later, it's time for a long siesta.

Wine Pairing

Guado al Tasso Vermentino, Toscana

Serves 2-4

· 8 oz *linguine*
· 4 tablespoons extra-virgin olive oil
· 2 garlic cloves, thinly sliced
· *Peperoncino*, to taste
· 1/3 cup dry white wine
· 2 1/2 pound littleneck clams
  (around 50 clams) washed
· 2 teaspoon Italian parsley, finely minced

Directions

Bring 4 quarts of "lightly" salted water to boil in a large pot. There is plenty of salt in the clams.

In a 12" frying pan, heat olive oil over medium-low heat. Add garlic and *peperoncino* and cook slowly until fragrant, about 30 seconds. Add wine and clams; raise heat to medium-high and cover. Give the pan a good shake from time to time. Remove clams as they open and transfer to a bowl. Clams will take about 5-6 minutes to open. At this point, you can, if you wish, remove the clams from their shells. I like to leave a few clams in their shells to decorate the pasta once it's plated.

Add pasta to the boiling water and cook just shy of *al dente*. Using tongs or a pasta fork, transfer pasta from the pot directly into the frying pan. Add 1/3 cup of pasta water to the pan and cook pasta 1-2 minutes over high heat, tossing the pasta or shaking the pan while whisking the pasta with tongs. Keep things moving to create a velvety emulsified sauce. If the emulsion breaks down, add a few tablespoons of pasta water and keep tossing until the emulsion reappears. Add clams and liquid from bowl into the frying pan and toss with parsley.

Twirl the *linguine* into nests on warm plates; garnish with clams still in their shells.

Malloreddus alla Campidanese
Sardinian Gnocchi with Sausage Ragù

Sardinia is an astoundingly beautiful island with over one thousand miles of Mediterranean shoreline. It also boasts some of the best beaches in Italy. While fish is on the menu all over the coast, meat takes center stage in the interior of the island. That's where you'll find donkey steaks and wild boar *prosciutto*. Sucking pig and lamb can be found roasting with wild fennel at *agriturismi* (farmhouses converted into inns and restaurants) throughout the island. What you eat on these farms is grown and produced on them. Whether you stay at one of the many *agriturismi* or not, they are worth a visit for an excellent and authentic Sardinian meal. Some *agriturismi* even offer cooking classes. Sa Madra outside Alghero offers an excellent Sardinian dining experience.

Wine Pairing

Cantina Oliena Cannonau di Sardegna "Nepente," Sardegna

4-6 portions

· 16 oz fresh *malloreddus*
· 2 tablespoons extra-virgin olive oil
· 2 garlic cloves, crushed
· *Peperoncino*, to taste
· 1 yellow onion, finely chopped
· 1/2 pound pork or lamb sausage, casings removed
· 14 oz can of San Marzano tomatoes (crushed with your hands)
· 1/4 cup red wine
· 1 bay leaf
· Salt, to taste
· Black pepper, freshly ground to taste
· 1 teaspoon fennel seeds
· 1 pinch saffron
· 8-12 whole basil leaves
· 1/4 cup *Fiori Sardo* (aged *pecorino* from Sardinia), freshly grated

Directions

Bring 4 quarts of salted water to boil in a large pot.

In a 12" frying pan, heat the olive oil, garlic, and *peperoncino* over medium-low heat and cook until fragrant; remove garlic. Increase heat to medium; add chopped onion and cook for five minutes until translucent. Add the sausage to the onions, breaking up the meat with a wooden spoon, and brown. Add tomatoes and their sauce, wine, bay leaf, salt, pepper, fennel seeds, and saffron. Simmer uncovered over low heat for 45 minutes.

Add *malloreddus* to the boiling water and cook for 5-8 minutes until tender (check by tasting). Drain pasta into the frying pan with a kitchen spider. Add 1-2 tablespoons of pasta water to loosen and emulsify the sauce. Stir and toss rapidly to marry the pasta with the sauce.

Serve on warm plates; garnish with a couple of small basil leaves and freshly grated *Fiori Sardo*.

Orecchiette con Cime di Rapa
Orecchiette with Broccoli Rabe

On any given day in Bari Vecchia, the historic old town of Bari, you can find a dozen or so *Nonne* or grandmothers making hand-made *orecchiette* on the narrow streets outside their homes near the Basilica San Nicola. Kneading and rolling semolina dough with their hands and a knife on rough wooden boards, these women can make several pounds of pasta in an hour, which they bag and sell to local residents, restaurants, and tourists. The first time I walked down the Via dell'Arco Basso and the Via dell'Arco Alto, where these women work side by side, I was fascinated by the photographic opportunities. I was reluctant, however; I didn't want them to feel exploited. I later learned about Valentina Piccinni's book of photographs called the *Pasta Divas of Bari*. When I returned to Bari a year later, I gathered the courage to ask one of the women if I could film her with my iPhone while she worked, just her hands I assured her. To my surprise, she insisted that I show her face. I later found out that her name is Nunzia and that she is quite well known because of numerous YouTube videos and appearances on national television. She will even cook *orecchiette con cime di rapa* for you in her kitchen. If you like bitter greens, you'll love this classic dish from Puglia.

Wine Pairing

Felline Fiano Salento, Puglia

2-4 portions

· 8 oz fresh orecchiette
· 3 tablespoons extra-virgin olive oil
· 1 garlic clove, crushed
· *Peperoncino*, to taste
· 2 anchovy fillets
· 12 ounces *cime di rapa*
· Salt, to taste
· 1/4 cup panko bread crumbs
· *Pecorino Pugliese*, freshly grated (optional)

Directions

In a small frying pan, heat 1 tablespoon of olive oil over medium heat. Add bread crumbs and sauté until brown; set aside.

Bring 6 quarts of salted water to boil in a large pot.

Add *cime di rapa* to the boiling water and cook for 3 minutes. Remove *cime di rapa* with a kitchen spider and plunge into a salad spinner filled with ice water bath. Drain and spin until dry. Roughly chop and set aside.

In a 10" frying pan, heat olive oil, garlic, *peperoncino*, and anchovies over medium-low heat and cook until fragrant, about 2-3 minutes. Be careful not to let the garlic brown. Add *cima di rape* until warm and remove from heat.

Add orecchiette to the boiling water and cook until it rises to the surface. Remove pasta with a kitchen spider and add to frying pan with the cima di rapa. Toss over medium heat until coated.

Transfer pasta to warm plates; drizzle with a little extra-virgin olive oil and garnish with bread crumbs and/or *Pecorino Pugliese*.

Paccheri all'Amatriciana di Mare
Paccheri with Cured Pork Cheek, Tomatoes and Seafood

This is a popular pasta dish from the Lazio region of Italy. I first tried it at Pierluigi several years ago, at what has since become my favorite seafood restaurant in Rome. Located on the Piazza de' Ricci between the Via del Pellegrino and the Via Guilia, Pierluigi has been around for over eighty years. Once you've been seated in one of the elegant dining rooms or outdoors on the piazza, you will be invited by your waiter to go look at the beautiful display of fresh fish and shellfish. The chef standing behind the display will recommend the various ways that your selection should be cooked. This is my adaptation of their *paccheri all'amatriciana di mare*. The dish is a bit unusual in that it includes both *guanciale* and *Pecorino Romano*.

Wine Pairing

Casale del Gigilio Bellone, Lazio

Serves 2-4

· 8 oz *paccheri* or *mezzi paccheri*
· 1 tablespoon extra-virgin olive oil
· 1 oz *guanciale*, cut into thin slices
· 1 large shallot, finely minced
· 2 garlic cloves, crushed
· *Peperoncino*, to taste
· 8 oz canned cherry tomatoes in their sauce
· 12 littleneck clams, washed
· 12 mussels, washed and debearded
· 1/4 cup dry white wine
· 4 *calamari* tubes, cut into thin rings, and four tentacles
· 4 shrimp, shelled, deveined, and diced
· 4 large head-on shrimp
· 4 large sea scallops, cut in half crosswise
· 1/2 pound monkfish, cut into 1/2" pieces
· Salt, to taste
· White pepper, freshly ground to taste
· *Pecorino Romano*, optional
· Basil leaves to garnish

Directions

Bring 4 quarts of salted water to boil in a large pot.

In a 12" frying pan, heat olive oil, *guanciale*, minced shallot, garlic, and *peperoncino* over medium-low heat until the guanciale has rendered its fat and shallots are soft. Be patient; avoid the temptation to turn up the heat. When the *guanciale* and shallots are translucent, remove garlic cloves and discard.

Increase temperature to medium-high; add tomato sauce from the canned cherry tomatoes (reserve tomatoes until later). Add clams, mussels, and white wine and cover. Shake pan from time to time. Remove shellfish as they open. Mussels will open first. Remove meat from all but 4 mussels and 4 clams.

Add *calamari*; cover and cook over medium heat for 2-3 minutes. Add shrimp, scallops, monkfish, and a pinch of salt. Reintroduce mussels and clams and reduce heat to low. Cook for 5 minutes

Add pasta to the boiling water and cook until *al dente*. Using tongs or a pasta fork, transfer pasta from the pot directly into the frying pan. Add pasta water as needed to loosen the sauce. Cook 2-3 minutes over high heat, tossing the pasta or shaking the pan while spooning sauce over the pasta. Keep things moving to create a velvety emulsified sauce. If the emulsion breaks down, add a little more pasta water and keep tossing until the emulsion reappears.

Divide pasta and seafood evenly on warm plates. Top with some freshly ground white pepper, drizzle a little extra-virgin olive oil, and add a few basil leaves as a garnish. Grate a little *Pecorino Romano*, if you wish. Cheese is allowed with this Roman dish.

Pappardelle al Ragù di Cinghiale
Pappardelle with Wild Boar Ragù

In addition to feeding my students rabbit and wild hare during Dominican University's Summer-in-Florence program, I like to introduce them to wild boar, which are hunted throughout Tuscany. *Pappardelle al ragù di cinghiale* is considered a regional specialty and it's delicious. I love its gamey, earthy flavor. I buy my *cinghiale* from a butcher in the *Mercato Centrale* that specializes in wild game. His sparse stall offers a few hunks of wild boar, a few rabbits, and, on occasion, a large blood-red wild hare worthy of being painted by Soutine. This one-man butcher shop stands in marked contrast to the Alimentari Perini across the aisle with its numerous hams hanging from the ceiling, cured meats, cheeses, pasta sauces, and bustling traffic. Next stop in the *Mercato* is the fresh pasta stall, where I buy enough fresh yellow *pappardelle* to feed an army. Then, on to the vegetable stalls, where I pick up some fresh *porcini* mushrooms for my *ragú*. You have to be careful when buying fresh *porcini* mushrooms. Sometimes you might get one that's soft and rotted or one that contains tiny worms that don't make their appearance until you start cooking them.

I learned this lesson the hard way a few years ago when, after browning my *cinghiale*, I added my fresh *porcini*. Within seconds, dozens, if not hundreds, of tiny white worms, AKA larvae or maggots, began wiggling their way out of the dark crevices of the porcini mushrooms. In a panic, with three hours to spare until the students arrived, I frantically started to Google "What are those white worms in my mushrooms?"; "What are maggots"; "Are maggots poisonous?" By the time I had my answer that neither I nor my students or colleague were going to die from what is essentially eatable protein, the little white creatures had melted and disappeared into the braise. Another happy family dinner…

The following recipe can be divided proportionally. I also have substituted dried *porcini* mushrooms for fresh. I like their concentrated flavor, and they easier to obtain back home.

Wine Pairing

La Mozza Aragone, Toscana

Serves 12-16

- 8 cups chicken stock, preferably homemade
- 6 oz dried *porcini* mushrooms
- 4 pounds wild boar shoulder, diced into 1/2" cubes
- Salt, to taste
- Black pepper, freshly ground to taste
- 3/4 cup extra-virgin olive oil + additional if needed when browning meat
- 4 garlic cloves, finely sliced
- 1/2 teaspoon crushed *peperoncino*
- 4 medium yellow onions, minced
- 4 tablespoons parsley, finely chopped
- 4 tablespoons fresh rosemary, finely chopped
- 8 bay leaves
- 2 cups dry red wine
- 56 oz San Marzano tomatoes, crushed with your hands
- 3-4 pounds fresh *pappardelle*
- *Parmigiano Reggiano*, freshly grated

Directions

Heat chicken stock and pour 2 cups over dried *porcini* mushrooms to cover and let soak for 30 minutes. After the mushrooms have become soft, strain stock through a sieve and reserve mushroom liquid and mushrooms.

Season boar meat with salt and pepper. Heat olive oil in a large Dutch oven over medium-high heat and brown the meat in small batches. Be careful not to crowd the pan. Let the meat brown for at least five minutes before stirring. Remove browned meat with a slotted spoon to a large bowl and continue browning.

Reduce heat to medium and add garlic and *peperoncino*; cook for 30 seconds until fragrant. Add onions, *porcini* mushrooms, parsley, rosemary, and bay leaves, and cook for 20 minutes until onions are translucent and soft.

Return meat back to the pot; add wine, stir, and cook uncovered until wine has evaporated.

Add tomatoes, chicken broth, and mushroom liquid and reduce to low. Simmer gently with the lid slightly askew for about two hours. Stir occasionally. Check salt and pepper seasoning.

Bring 8 quarts of salted water to boil in a 12-quart stock pot.

Add pasta to the boiling water in batches and cook *al dente*, about two minutes. Fresh pasta will cook very fast.

Use a kitchen spider to remove and drain pasta and add to a warm serving plate or bowl. Ladle some of the *ragú* over each batch. Serve with freshly grated *Parmigiano Reggiano* and a drizzle of good extra-virgin olive oil.

Pasta alla Puttanesca

Pasta alla Puttanesca

This aromatic, assertive dish was invented in Naples. It's been said that *puttane* (prostitutes) would make it in order to lure customers, or that it was a dish they could quickly make between customers. Who knows? I like it because it's made with some of my favorite staples that I always have on hand and that don't need refrigeration – pasta, tomatoes, anchovies, capers, and olives. It's also a dish that can come together in 15-20 minutes, making it a perfect dish after a long day of teaching.

Wine Pairing

De Angelis Lacrima Christi del Vesuvio, Campania

Serves 2-4

· 8 oz dried long pasta, such as *spaghetti* or *linguine*
· 1 tablespoon extra-virgin olive oil
· 8 anchovies
· 1/2 teaspoon *peperoncino*
· 4 cloves of garlic, thinly sliced
· 14 oz can of whole San Marzano tomatoes, crushed
· 1/4 cup *Gaeta* or *Niçoise* olives, pitted
· 2 tablespoons capers, drained
· Salt, to taste
· Black pepper, freshly ground to taste
· Fresh basil to garnish

Directions

Bring 4 quarts of salted water to boil in a large pot.

In a 12" frying pan, heat olive oil and anchovies over medium-low heat for a minute or two; break up the anchovies with a wooden spoon. Add garlic and *peperoncino* and cook about 30 seconds until fragrant. Add tomatoes, olives, capers, salt, and black pepper and cook over medium heat for 10 minutes until sauce thickens.

Add pasta to the boiling water and cook until pasta is just shy of *al dente*. Using tongs or a pasta fork, transfer pasta from the pot directly into the frying pan with the tomato sauce. Cook 2-3 minutes over medium heat, tossing the pasta or shaking the pan while whisking the pasta with tongs.

Serve on warm plates; garnish with basil leaves.

Spaghetti Aglio, Olio e Peperoncino
Spaghetti with Garlic, Olive Oil and Red Pepper Flakes

Quando no c'è niente nel frigo - spaghetti, aglio, olio, e peperoncino

This classic late-night favorite is the perfect dish to practice your emulsifying, "finish the pasta in the pan", skills. When I'm in Rome, I buy my *peperoncino* at the open-air market in Campo de' Fiori. On the southeast corner of the market, you will find a large spice booth operated by Mauro Berardi. He sells all kinds of spices and spice mixtures packed in pointy-ended plastic bags that he swears will keep the spices fresh for two years in the refrigerator. "Don't put the spices in jars" he told me, "or they will dry out." In my experience this has proven to be true. Year after year the *peperoncino* that I bring home remain pliable and fragrant for months.

Wine Pairing
Falesco Est! Est! Est! di Montefiascone, Lazio

Serves 2-4
· 8 oz *spaghetti*
· 2 1/2 tablespoons extra-virgin olive oil
· 5 cloves garlic, thinly sliced
· 1/4 teaspoon *peperoncino*
· 1/2 cup Italian parsley, finely chopped
· Salt, to taste

Directions
Bring 4 quarts of salted water to a boil in a large pot.

In a 10" frying pan, heat the olive oil, garlic, and *peperoncino* over medium-low until fragrant, about 2-3 minutes. Be careful not to let the garlic brown. Add 1/4 cup parsley and remove from heat.

Add pasta to the boiling water and cook just shy of *al dente*. Two minutes before the pasta is cooked, ladle ¾ cup pasta water into the garlic olive oil sauce and bring to a boil.

Using tongs or a pasta fork, transfer the pasta from the pot directly into the frying pan. Cook 1-2 minutes over medium-high heat, tossing the pasta or shaking the pan while whisking the pasta with tongs. You really have to keep things moving to create a velvety emulsified sauce. If the emulsion breaks down, add 2-3 tablespoons of pasta water at a time and keep tossing until the emulsion reappears.

Serve on warm plates. This is a thin sauce; you're not going to be able to twirl this dish into a tall tower. No cheese please.

Spaghetti ai Ricci di Mare
Spaghetti with Sea Urchin

The first time I ate *spaghetti ai ricci di mare* was at the Ristorante Trattoria Maristella in Alghero, Sardegna. This is a charming restaurant outside the historic center and is very popular with the locals. All of their seafood dishes are very fresh and in season. Having had *Uni* in Sushi restaurants, I figured it would be a great combination with spicy, garlicky pasta. Much like oysters, sea urchins taste briny like the sea, yet sweet at the same time. Their texture is creamy and custard-like. Who would think this spiny porcupine of the sea would contain such deliciousness.

Wine Pairing
Pala Vermentino di Sardegna "Stellato," Sardegna

Serves 2-4
· 8 oz spaghetti
· 3 tablespoons extra-virgin olive oil
· 3 garlic cloves, thinly sliced
· *Peperoncino*, to taste
· 10 pieces of sea urchin (about 3 oz)
· 1 tablespoon Italian parsley, finely chopped

Directions
Bring 4 quarts of lightly salted water to boil in a large pot.

In a 12" frying pan, heat olive oil over low heat; add garlic and *peperoncino* and cook until fragrant. Be careful not to let the garlic brown. Add half the sea urchin and cook over medium-low heat until pieces begin to break apart. Add parsley and remove from heat.

Add pasta to the boiling water and cook just shy of *al dente*. Using tongs or a pasta fork, transfer pasta from the pot directly into the frying pan. Add 1/2 cup pasta water and toss the pasta over medium-high heat until well-coated and emulsified.

Serve on warm plates with remaining sea urchin on top of the pasta.

Spaghetti al Nero di Seppia
Spaghetti with Squid Ink

I love Venice and have been going there for over twenty-five years. These days I usually go in mid-October to see either the *Biennale Arte* or the *Biennale Architettura*. It's a great time to visit; the crowds are smaller, the weather is a little cooler, and the city is decked out for the Venice marathon with ramps running up and down the stone bridges along the Riva degli Schiavoni. It's also almost certain that parts of the city will flood due to the high tides. Photos from the 2018 marathon show the athletes running in knee-deep water during sections of the race.

On my first night in Venice, after a *Negroni* and some *cicchetti* (Italian tapas) at El Sbarlefo in Cannaregio, I always go to the Ristorante Vecia Cavana near the Campo Santi Apostoli, where I order their *spaghetti al nero di seppia* and their grilled *coda di rospo* (monkfish) served with little more than a wedge of lemon on the side.

Wine Pairing
Cantina Prà Soave Classico "Otto," Veneto

Serves 2-4
· 8 oz *spaghetti*
· 3 tablespoons extra-virgin olive oil
· 2 garlic cloves, thinly sliced
· *Peperoncino*, to taste
· 1/2 pound *calamari* (tubes and tentacles). Cut the tubes lengthwise into thin strips.
· 3 tablespoons dry white wine
· 2 tablespoons cuttlefish ink (available online and at Eataly in small 3.2 oz jars)
· 6 oz San Marzano tomatoes, crushed with your hands
· 2-3 tablespoons Italian parsley, finely chopped

Directions
Bring 4 quarts of salted water to boil in a large pot.

In a 10" frying pan, heat the olive oil over low heat; add garlic and peperoncino and cook until fragrant. Be careful not to let the garlic brown. Increase heat to medium; add calamari and sauté for a 2-3 minutes until opaque. Add wine and simmer for 1-2 minutes.

Mix cuttlefish ink with a tablespoon or two of hot pasta water, and pour into the frying pan. Cover and simmer gently for 10 minutes. Add the tomatoes and their juice and continue simmering (covered) for another 10 minutes.

While the sauce is simmering, add pasta to the boiling water and cook just shy of *al dente*. Using tongs or a pasta fork, transfer the pasta from the pot directly into the sauce. I like my sauce thick so the pasta will hold its shape when I twirl it on my plate. If the sauce is too thick, however, you can always add a few tablespoons of pasta water. Continue cooking pasta in the simmering sauce (uncovered) for 2-3 minutes until pasta is tender but still *al dente*. Stir in half the parsley. Serve on warm plates and garnish with remaining parsley.

Spaghetti alla Bottarga
Spaghetti with Bottarga

The first time I tried spaghetti *alla bottarga* was several years ago while I was on vacation in Sardegna, in the beautiful medieval city of Alghero. I was very eager to try *bottarga* because Anthony Bourdain was so excited about it in his Sardinian episode of *No Reservations*. It did not disappoint. I first had it on *spaghetti*, then sprinkled over *linguine alle vongole*, then on a pizza with artichokes, and finally sliced and drizzled with olive oil on *pane carasau*, the traditional thin crispy flatbread from Sardegna. *Bottarga* has a briny delicate taste, with an explosion of *umami* flavor and hints of fishiness, a little like cavier or sea urchin. It's the salted and dried egg roe of either tuna or grey mullet. I prefer the subtle amber colored *bottarga di muggine* from the grey mullet. The best quality comes from the small town of Cabras in western Sardegna, where mullet is fished in the nearby brackish lagoons. In Rome, there is a shop called La Peonia on the Via delle Carroze near the Spanish steps where you can buy all kinds of *bottarga* and Sardinian delicacies. Whenever I'm in Rome, I always make a stop there to pick up a couple of 500-gram bags of grated *bottarga* to bring back home.

Wine Pairing
Cantina Mesa Vermentino
di Sardegna "Giunco," Sardegna

Serves 2-4
· 8 oz *spaghetti*
· 2 1/2 tablespoons extra-virgin olive oil
· 1 clove garlic, thinly sliced
· *Peperoncino*, to taste
· 2 oz whole *bottarga*, thinly sliced
  (a truffle slicer works well for this)
· 2 tablespoons *bottarga*, grated

Directions
Bring 4 quarts of lightly salted water to boil in a large pot. Bottarga contains plenty of salt.

In a 10" frying pan, heat olive oil over low heat; add garlic and *peperoncino* and cook until fragrant. Remove from heat and set aside.

Add pasta to the boiling water and cook just shy of *al dente*. Using tongs or a pasta fork, transfer pasta from the pot directly into the frying pan. Toss the pasta until well coated. Add pasta water by the tablespoon to create an emulsion. Add sliced *bottarga* in the pan off the heat. You don't want to cook *bottarga*.

Serve on warm plates and garnish with grated *bottarga*.

Spaghetti alle Capesante
Spaghetti with Scallops

Scallops are among of my favorite shellfish; I love their sweet, buttery, delicate taste. What you are eating is actually the adductor muscle that opens and closes the two shells. Highly nutritious, rich in protein, and low in calories, scallops were popular in both Greece and Rome. There are several mosaics from Pompeii in the Archeological Museum in Naples depicting these delicious bivalves. In Italy, they are called *capesante* ("holy shells") or *conchiglie di San Giacomo* – the grooved lines in the shells representing the various routes travelled by pilgrims around the world to the tomb of San Giacomo in Santiago de Compostella, Spain. It is said that San Giacomo used a scallop shell to beg for food during his own pilgrimage.

Scallops are widespread in the Mediterranean, especially in the Adriatic Sea. They cost about 10 Euros a kilo at the famed Rialto Fish Market in Venice. Although tomatoes are often added to this classic dish, my pasta recipe is *in bianco* (without tomatoes).

Wine Pairing

Agricola Inama Vigneti di Foscarino Soave Classico DOC, Veneto

Serves 2-4

- 8 oz *spaghetti*
- 1 tablespoon extra-virgin olive oil
- 12 large sea scallops, sliced in half crosswise
- 1 tablespoon unsalted butter
- 1 garlic clove, thinly sliced
- *Peperoncino*, to taste
- 1 cup dry white wine
- Salt, to taste
- White pepper, freshly ground to taste
- 1 tablespoon Italian parsley, finely chopped
- Zest from one lemon

Directions

Bring 4 quarts of salted water to boil in a large pot.

In a 12" frying pan, heat olive oil over medium-high heat until oil is almost smoking. Add scallops and sear for 2 minutes without touching them. Flip scallops over and sear the other side for 1-2 minutes; remove from pan and set aside.

Let pan cool for a few minutes. Over low heat, add butter, garlic, and *peperoncino* and cook until fragrant. Be careful not to let the garlic brown. Increase heat to high, add wine, and reduce for 1-2 minutes. Add salt, pepper, and parsley; remove from heat.

Add pasta to the boiling water and cook just shy of *al dente*. Using tongs or a pasta fork, transfer pasta from the pot directly into the frying pan. Toss the pasta and scallops over medium-high heat until well-coated and emulsified. If the emulsion breaks, add an ounce or two of pasta water to re-emulsify the sauce.

Serve on warm plates, distributing the scallops evenly on top of the pasta.

Spaghettoni alla Carbonara
Thick Spaghetti with Guanciale, Egg Yolks, Cheese, and Black Pepper

Spaghetti alla Carbonara is a classic Roman pasta dish, along with *pasta alla gricia, cacio e pepe,* and *pasta all'Amatriciana.* As with the others, there's a right way of making it and a wrong way. This dish should never include cream. Although pancetta can be used instead of *guanciale,* it is traditional to use cured hog's jowls. I like using the thicker *spaghettone* made by Afeltra for this dish, as it holds up to the bold, earthy flavors of the *guanciale* and *Pecorino Romano.* This is hearty comfort food, best enjoyed on a cold winter day.

Wine Pairing
Fontana Candida Frascati Superiore Riserva Luna Mater, Lazio

Serves 2-4
· 8 oz spaghettoni (*rigatoni* is also often used)
· 1 tablespoon extra-virgin olive oil
· 4 oz *guanciale,* cut into 1/4" thick lardons about 2" long
· 2 egg yolks (at room temperature)
· 1/2 cup *Pecorino Romano,* freshly grated
· 1 teaspoon black peppercorns, crushed (you really want them coarse for this dish; try crushing them with a cast iron frying pan on your cutting board).

Directions
Bring 4 quarts of salted water to boil in a large pot.

In a 12" frying pan, heat olive oil and *guanciale* over low heat and cook until the *guanciale* has rendered its fat and has become crispy. Be patient; avoid the temptation to turn up the heat. Turn off heat when done; remove 1/2 the guanciale and set aside for garnish.

In a bowl, mix egg yolks, *Pecorino Romano,* black pepper, and 2 tablespoons of pasta water and set aside.

Add pasta to the boiling water and cook just shy of *al dente.* Using tongs or a pasta fork, transfer pasta from the pot directly into the frying pan with the guanciale. Add 1/2 cup pasta water. Cook 2-3 minutes over medium-high heat, tossing the pasta or shaking the pan while whisking the pasta with tongs. If the emulsion breaks down, add a little more pasta water and keep tossing until the emulsion reappears.

Remove pan from heat and stir in egg yolk-cheese-and-black pepper mixture. Add additional pasta water by the tablespoon, if the sauce is too thick.

Serve on warm plates with crispy *guanciale* on top of each portion; add additional black pepper and grated *Pecorino Romano.*

Spaghettoni alla Gricia
Thick Spaghetti with Guanciale and Pecorino Romano

I teach a week-long course in Rome on Renaissance and Baroque Art during my university's winter interim. Over the years I have enjoyed curating the students' dining experiences as much as their art encounters. I work closely with our travel agency to ensure that the four classic Roman pastas: *pasta alla gricia*, *pasta all'Amatriciana*, *cacio e pepe*, and *spaghetti alla carbonara* make it on to the menus of our group meals. This is my version of *spaghetti alla gricia*. I like to use the thicker *spaghettoni* for this dish as it holds up to the bold, earthy flavors of the *guanciale* and *Pecorino Romano*. Romans often argue about the authenticity of their traditional dishes. Purists say no to the addition of onions, while others prefer the addition of onions. In my opinion, they add a touch of sweetness to the dish and add another layer of flavor. Last year's farewell dinner in Rome was held at the excellent EnOsteria Capolecase near the Piazza Barberini. The chef there tops off the pasta with crispy lardons of *guanciale*. As with the addition of the onions, they add another dimension and texture to this earthy dish.

Wine Pairing
Castello di Torre in Pietra Roma Rosso, Lazio

Serves 2-4
· 8 oz *spaghettoni*
· 1 tablespoon extra-virgin olive oil
· *Peperoncino*, to taste
· 4 oz *guanciale* cut into 1/4" thick lardons about 2" long
· 1 garlic clove, thinly sliced
· 1/2 small red onion trimmed and thinly sliced lengthwise (about 4 oz)
· Handful of whole Italian parsley leaves, stems removed
· 1/4 cup *Pecorino Romano*, freshly grated

Directions
Bring 4 quarts of salted water to boil in a large pot.

In a 12" frying pan, heat olive oil, *guanciale* and *peperoncino* over medium-low heat and cook until the guanciale has rendered it fat and has become crispy. Remove half the *guanciale* with a slotted spoon and set aside. Use these strips to garnish your pasta when you plate it. Drain all but a tablespoon of oil. Lower heat to low; add garlic and cook for 30 seconds until fragrant. Do not let it brown. Add onions and cook gently over low heat until onions are soft and translucent. Turn off the heat when done.

Add pasta to the boiling water and cook just shy of *al dente*. Using tongs or a pasta fork, transfer pasta from the pot directly into the frying pan. Add 4 oz of pasta water. Cook 1-2 minutes over medium-high heat, tossing the pasta or shaking the pan while whisking the pasta with tongs. Keep things moving to create a velvety emulsified sauce. If the emulsion breaks down, add a little more pasta water and keep tossing until the emulsion reappears.

Remove pan from heat; stir in *Pecorino Romano* and parsley leaves. Serve on warm plates with crispy *guanciale* and some additional *Pecorino Romano* on top of each portion.

Spaghettoni con le Sarde
Thick Spaghetti with Sardines

If there is one food item that can change my lunch or dinner plans, it's seeing fresh sardines at the market – the smaller the better. *Pasta con le Sarde* always comes to mind ever since I first enjoyed it at the Ristorante Charleston in Mondello near Palermo many years ago. More recently, I had an excellent version of this dish at the bright and colorful Siciliainbocca, located in the Prati neighborhood in Rome. My charming Airbnb hostess, Luisa Santarelli, highly recommended the restaurant. It has quickly become one of my favorite restaurants in Rome, far from the tourist sights and fast food traps.

Wine Pairing

Cantine Barbera Inzolia Menfi "Tivitti," Sicilia

Serves 2-4

· 8 oz *spaghettoni*
· 1/4 cup golden raisins
· 1/4 cup dry white wine
· 4 tablespoons extra-virgin olive oil
· 1 large shallot, finely minced
· 1 garlic clove, finely minced
· 1 small fennel bulb, finely minced
  (fronds chopped and reserved)
· *Peperoncino*, to taste
· 1 pound small sardines, cleaned and deboned
· 1/4 cup panko bread crumbs, browned
· 2 teaspoons fennel seeds, toasted and
  crushed
· Salt to taste
· 1/4 cup pine nuts, toasted
· 2 tablespoon salted capers, rinsed

Directions

Bring 4 quarts of salted water to boil in a large pot.

Cover raisins with the wine and set aside to soften. In a small frying pan, brown the bread crumbs with 2 tablespoon of olive oil; remove to a small plate.

In a 12" frying pan, heat 3 tablespoons of olive oil and sauté the shallot, garlic, fennel, and *peperoncino*. Add salt to taste and cook until fennel is soft and shallots are translucent. Add wine, raisins, and sardines to the vegetables and cook over low heat for 10 minutes. Add a little salted water if needed.

Add pasta to the boiling water and cook just shy of *al dente*.

Using tongs or a pasta fork, transfer pasta from the pot directly into the frying pan with the sardines and fennel. Mix gently; add salt and pepper to taste.

Serve on warm plates; garnish with fennel fronds, fennel seeds, pine nuts, capers, bread crumbs, and a touch of olive oil.

Tagliatelle alla Bolognese
Tagliatelle with Bolognese Sauce

Bologna is a sophisticated city known for its churches, nine-hundred year old university, leaning towers, and twenty-five miles of *portici* (porticoes) that cover the city's sidewalks. Bologna is also known for its food and is considered the culinary capital of Italy.

Many summers ago, while teaching in Florence, I took my students on a drawing field trip to Bologna. We took the train, which, back then, took about an hour. After taking in Morandi's paintings and the recreation of his studio in the Palazzo Communale, we headed to the Basilica di Santo Stefano, where we spent the afternoon drawing in the cloisters. That summer, I had a large group of very talented students from Arizona State University, Purdue, and Dominican University. After class, we headed to a local *trattoria* to eat, among other things, *Tagliatelle alla Bolognese*. It was a memorable meal, if somewhat chaotic, with 24 students. As we were finishing our coffee, I asked the owner if he would check the train schedule back to Florence. He informed me that the last train had just departed and that the next train wouldn't depart until 6:00am the next morning. When I informed the students, their faces lit up in anticipation of the adventure they were about to experience. We decided to stay together as a group and drink some wine in a café under one of the porticoes. Some students even continued to draw. When that café closed, we moved to another bar; when that one closed, yet another, until they were all closed. Finally, around two in the morning, we returned to the train station where we slept, or tried to sleep, on the benches outside the station. The next morning, we took the first train back to Florence and arrived just in time for morning classes. The students were excited and happy with their adventure – my colleagues and university president, not so much.

Wine Pairing

Villa Bagnolo Sangiovese di Romagna
Superiore "Sassetto", Emilia-Romagna

Serves 4-6

· 1 tablespoon extra-virgin olive oil
· 3 oz pancetta, finely chopped
· 4 garlic cloves, finely chopped
· 1/4 teaspoon *peperoncino*
· 1 onion, finely chopped
· 1 carrot, peeled and finely chopped
· 1 celery rib, finely chopped
· 8 oz ground pork
· 8 oz ground veal or beef
· 1 teaspoon fresh thyme leaves, chopped
· Salt, to taste
· Black pepper, to taste
· 4 tablespoons *doppio concentrato di pomodoro* (double-concentrated tomato paste)
· 1 cup dry white wine
· 1/2 cup whole milk
· 16 oz fresh egg *tagliatelle*
· 1/4 cup Italian parsley, finely chopped
· *Parmigiano Reggiano*, freshly grated

Directions

Heat olive oil in a 4-6 quart sauce pan over medium heat. Add *pancetta* and cook until it has rendered its fat. Add garlic and *peperoncino* and cook for 30 seconds, until fragrant. Add chopped onion, carrot, and celery and cook until soft, about 5 minutes. Increase heat to medium-high and add ground pork and veal; break the meat up with a wooden spoon. Add thyme, salt, pepper, and white wine; reduce wine by half. Add tomato paste and milk and simmer over very low heat for 1 1/2 hours.

Bring 8 quarts of salted water to boil in a 12-quart stock pot. Add pasta to the boiling water and cook *al dente*, about one minute. Fresh pasta will cook very fast. When the pasta is cooked, use a kitchen spider to transfer pasta to the sauce pan and allow pasta to finish cooking in the sauce for about 1 minute. If the sauce seems dry, add a little pasta water.

Serve on warm plates with chopped parsley and freshly grated *Parmigiano*.

Trofie al Pesto con Patate e Fagiolini
Trofie with Pesto, Potatoes and Beans

This is a classic Ligurian summer pasta. I've eaten it many times from Riomaggiore to Monterosso al Mare and beyond. At its best, it's prepared with handmade *trofie* pasta, *pesto al basilico*, thin *haricots verts*, and waxy potatoes. It's the perfect *primo* before a plate of fresh grilled fish, grilled octopus, or braised rabbit.

Wine Pairing
Cantine Lunae Bosoni Vermentino Colli di Luni (Grey Label), Liguria

Serves 2-4
· 8 oz trofie pasta (fresh or dried)
· 1/4 cup yellow potatoes, peeled and cut into 1/2" cubes
· 1/4 cup thin *haricots verts*, cut in 1" lengths
· 1/2 cup prepared basil pesto
· *Parmigiano Reggiano*, freshly grated

Directions
Bring 4 quarts of salted water to boil in a large pot. Add beans and potatoes and cook for 6-8 minutes until tender. Remove and set aside in a warm bowl.

Add *trofie* pasta to the boiling water and cook *al dente*. Transfer pasta into a warm bowl with a kitchen spider. Add beans and potatoes and mix in pesto. Add 1-2 of tablespoons of pasta water if sauce is dry.

Divide onto warm plates and garnish with additional *Parmigiano Reggian*o.

Pesto alla Genovese
Basil Pesto

Ingredients
· 2 cups basil leaves, stems removed (approx. 2 oz)
· 3 garlic cloves, chopped
· 1/2 cup pine nuts
· 1/2 teaspoon kosher salt
· 1/2 teaspoon white pepper, freshly ground
· 1/2 cup extra-virgin olive oil
· 1/2 cup *Pecorino Toscano* aged 6 months, freshly grated
· 1/2 cup *Parmigiano Reggiano*, freshly grated

Directions
Place basil, garlic, pine nuts, salt, and pepper in the bowl of a food processor and puree. Slowly add olive oil while processing. Add *Pecorino Toscano* and *Parmigiano Reggiano* and pulse; check for salt.

PRIMI—RISO

Paella di Mare
Seafood Paella

Although *paella* is a Spanish dish originating from Valencia, it's loved by everyone. I make it a lot and love experimenting with different seafood combinations. Sometimes I'll make a mixed *paella* with seafood and chicken. Occasionally I'll make *arroz negro* with squid ink. Sometimes I'm in the mood for a rabbit or duck *paella*. The secret to good *paella* is to remember it's all about the rice and the broth, which should always be homemade if possible. Also, don't overload the pan with protein. My rule of thumb is to use 1 pound of protein for each cup of rice. I have several *paella* pans in different sizes. The recipe below requires a 16" *paella* pan, but you could cut the recipe in half and use a 12" frying pan. Likewise, if you have a 20" pan, you could triple the ingredients, cutting back a bit on the olive oil. The best *paella* pans are made from carbon steel that doesn't warp. I buy mine from La Tienda, the online store specializing in Spanish foods and cooking equipment.

Wine Pairing

Feudi di San Gregorio Greco di Tufo, Campania

Serves 4

· 1/2 cup extra-virgin olive oil
· 2 garlic cloves, minced
· *Peperoncino*, to taste
· 1/2 cup yellow onion, chopped
· 1/2 cup San Marzano tomatoes, crushed
· 1 1/2 pounds mixed seafood
  (squid, scallops, shelled shrimp, etc.)
· 1/2 pound firm white fish, such as
  Monkfish (cut into 1" pieces)
· 1 teaspoon *Pimentón de La Vera*
  (spicy or sweet; I like it spicy)
· 1 bay leaf
· 1/2 teaspoon thyme
· 2 cups *Arborio* rice
· 1/2 cup dry white wine
· 1 teaspoon saffron threads
· 3 1/2 cups fish broth + additional if needed
· 8 littleneck clams
· 12 small mussels
· Sea salt, to taste
· 1 tablespoon Italian parsley, finely chopped

Directions

Heat 3 1/2 cups of fish broth and bring to a simmer. Pulverize saffron threads and add to broth; keep warm.

Add olive oil to the *paella* pan with garlic and *peperoncino* over low heat. Cook until fragrant, making sure not to brown. Add chopped onions, tomatoes, *pimentón*, bay leaf, and thyme and continue cooking over low until onions and tomatoes are translucent and jammy. This is your *soffritto* or base.

Next, add the mixed seafood and sauté for 3-4 minutes over medium-high heat. Stir in rice and cook for 2 minutes over medium heat until the rice becomes opaque. Add white wine and cook down for 2-3 minutes over medium heat. Tuck mussels and clams into the rice so that they open upwards. Add saffron infused fish broth; increase heat to medium-high and cook for 20 minutes.

Keep a close eye on the pan; you may have to lower the heat toward the end of cooking or rotate the pan over two burners. Never stir *paella*; it is not *risotto*. Towards the end of cooking take a spoon and carefully check the bottom of the pan for the crispy caramelized bottom called *socarrat*. This is the best part of the dish!

Once the *paella* is cooked, sprinkle with minced parsley, cover loosely with tin foil, and let rest for ten minutes before serving.

Risotto ai Frutti di Mare
Seafood Risotto

I generally don't eat a lot of rice when I'm in Italy. I don't know why, because I like it. Perhaps, it's because it's not as photogenic as pasta. It doesn't have the seductive curls of long pasta or the infinitely interesting geometric forms of the short handmade pastas. Rice just kind of melts onto the plate, much like polenta. Both can be delicious, however. Making *risotto* is only slightly more process-oriented than making paella, but not by much. The Ristorante La Cambusa in Positano makes a particularly good *risotto alla pescatora*. You can make this dish with any combination of shellfish you like, such as clams, mussels, *calamari*, octopus, shrimp, or lobster. Just keep the proportions approximately the same.

Wine Pairing

Marisa Cuomo Ravello Bianco, Campania

Serves 4

· 3 tablespoons extra-virgin olive oil
· 2 garlic cloves, minced
· *Peperoncino*, to taste
· 1 1/4 cup of dry white wine
· 16 littleneck clams, scrubbed
· 16 mussels, scrubbed and debearded
· 12 medium raw shrimp, peeled and deveined
· 5 cups fish stock (or clam juice)
· 3 tablespoons unsalted butter
· 1 cup shallots, finely chopped
· Salt, to taste
· 2 cups *Arborio* rice
· 2 whole San Marzano tomatoes from a can, drained and crushed
· White pepper, freshly ground
· 2 tablespoons Italian parsley, finely minced

Directions

Over low heat in a 12" frying pan, sauté 1 minced garlic clove and *peperoncino* in 1 tablespoon of olive oil until translucent and fragrant. Add 1/4 cup white wine, clams, and mussels; cover and raise heat to medium-high. Shake pan from time to time. Mussels will open up first (within 2-3 minutes); remove to a bowl and re-cover the pan. Remove clams as they open (another 2-3 minutes) and add to mussels with their juice; remove pan from heat. Shell mussels and clams, reserving 4 of each, still in their shells, for garnishing dishes.

Heat stock; reduce to simmer and cover.

Add 1 tablespoon of olive oil and 1 tablespoon of butter to frying pan with a pinch of salt and sauté remaining garlic and shallots over low heat until translucent and fragrant. Add rice; increase heat to medium and stir until opaque (approximately 3-4 minutes). Add remaining white wine and cook over medium heat until evaporated (2-3 minutes). Add tomatoes, the liquid from the shelled mussels and clams, another pinch of salt, and 1/2 cup stock. Stir constantly until liquid has evaporated. Add another ½ cup of stock; check for salt and keep stirring. Continue until you have incorporated 4 cups of broth plus wine.

Add the shrimp and remaining stock and cook over medium heat 4 minutes. Taste for salt and texture. If risotto is too stiff, add additional stock. Add remaining tablespoon of olive oil, 2 tablespoons of butter, and shelled mussels and clams. Stir well; add salt and white pepper to taste.

Plate in warmed bowls, garnish with shrimp, one unshelled clam, and one unshelled mussel. Add minced parsley and serve immediately.

Risotto al Nero di Seppia
Risotto with Cuttlefish Ink

This is a delicious cousin to *spaghetti al nero di sepia*. It has the same *umami* flavors from the cuttlefish ink and tomatoes. The Venetians like their *risotto al nero di sepia to be all'onda*, or wavelike. Traditionally it is served on a plate and not in a bowl.

Wine Pairing

Serafini & Vidotto Pinot Nero, Veneto

Serves 4-6
· 1/4 cup extra virgin olive oil
· 1 yellow onion, finely chopped
· 2 garlic cloves, sliced
· 12 ounces baby cuttlefish cut in half, or squid into thin strips
· 2 teaspoons cuttlefish ink or squid ink
· 1/2 cup dry white wine
· 8 ounces whole San Marzano tomatoes, crushed by hand
· Salt, to taste
· Black pepper, freshly ground to taste
· 1/2 stick unsalted butter
· 2 cups *Arborio* rice
· 5 cups fish stock
· Italian parsley, finely chopped

Directions

Heat fish stock in a sauce pan over low heat.

In a 12" frying pan heat the olive oil with half the onion over medium heat. Cook until soft and translucent. Add garlic, cuttlefish, and cuttlefish ink; cook for five minutes. Add wine, tomatoes, salt, and pepper. Cover and simmer for 30-45 minutes until cuttlefish is tender.

In another 12" frying pan, sauté the other half of the onion with the butter over medium heat. Add rice and toast for 2 minutes. Add 1 cup of stock; stir until rice absorbs the stock. Repeat with another half cup of stock. Keep adding stock until rice has cooked for 8 minutes.

After 8 minutes transfer rice to the cuttlefish sauce and continue to cook over medium heat, stirring often. Add stock or water as needed. After cooking 16-18 minutes, the *risotto* should be *al dente* or toothsome in a creamy sauce. You want this *risotto* is be slightly soupy.

Stir vigorously off heat to emulsify the rice with the oil and liquid, and pour *risotto* onto a warm flat plate. Garnish with parsley.

Risotto allo Zafferano
Saffron Risotto

I love the simplicity of this dish. It's a perfect combination of modest ingredients. Most recipes for this risotto use the same items and proportions. It's the ultimate comfort food. It can be a *primo*, a *secondo*, or a *contorno*. It's a great companion to *stinco di agnello*, braised lamb shanks, or *osso buco*, (braised veal shanks). I encourage you to make your own chicken stock – you will be deeply rewarded.

Wine Pairing

Cà dei Frati Lugana "I Frati," Lombardia

Serves 2-4
· 1 1/2 quarts homemade chicken stock
· 1 teaspoon saffron threads
· 1/4 cup extra-virgin olive oil
· 2 large shallots, finely minced
· 1 1/2 cups *Arborio* rice
· 1/2 cup dry white wine
· 3 tablespoon cold unsalted butter,
  cut into small pieces
· 1/2 cup *Parmigiano Reggiano*, freshly grated
· Salt, to taste

Directions

Heat the chicken stock over medium-high heat until warm; reduce to simmer. Add saffron threads to one cup of stock and set aside.

In a 10" frying pan sauté shallots in olive oil over low heat until translucent and fragrant. Add rice; increase heat to medium and stir until opaque (approximately 3-4 minutes). Add wine and the cup of stock with the dissolved saffron; stir with a wooden spoon until the rice has absorbed the liquid. Pour in another 1/2 cup of stock; stir and allow rice to absorb liquid. Continue adding 1/2 cup ladles of stock at a time until rice is creamy but still *al dente*. Check salt with a few kernels of rice every time you add more stock. This will give you a good idea of how cooked or *al dente* you want your *risotto*.

When done (about 15-20 minutes) remove pan from heat, add the cheese and butter and stir with a wooden spoon until well mixed. Add additional stock if needed. *Risotto* should be slightly soupy; you should be able to toss it in the pan up until the time you serve it in warm bowls, which should be immediately.

PRIMI—ZUPPE

Cacciucco alla Livornese
Tuscan Seafood Stew

Cacciucco is a delicious, satisfying seafood stew popular on the Tuscan coast from Livorno to Viareggio. As with most seafood stews, it was originally made by fisherman with the fish that did not sell on a given day. The more different kinds of fish used, the better. It's been said that *Cacciucco* needs at least five different kinds of fish and seafood – one for each 'c' in the spelling of he word. *Cacciucco* is unusual in that it includes octopus, tomatoes, and red wine. Because it can be difficult to eat without getting some of it on your clothes, many restaurants will provide you with a plastic bib, often with a kitschy bow tie printed on it. Although this is a coastal dish, it's not really beach food and is best eaten on a cool autumn or winter day.

Wine Pairing

Cecilia Elba Ansonica, Toscana

Serves 4

· 1/4 pound *calamari*, 1/4 tubes and 1/4 tentacles
· 1/4 pound shrimp, shelled and deveined
· 1/2 pound sea scallops, cut in half crosswise
· Salt, to taste
· White pepper, freshly ground to taste
· 1/4 cup extra-virgin olive oil
· 2 cloves garlic, finely sliced
· *Peperoncino*, to taste
· 1/2 onion, finely diced
· 2 pounds of large octopus tentacles or several small whole octopuses, heads removed
· 1 cup dry red wine
· 1/2 tablespoon double-concentrated tomato paste
· 14 oz can of San Marzano tomatoes, crushed
· 1/2 pound mussels, rinsed, scrubbed, and debearded
· 1/2 pound littleneck clams, rinsed and scrubbed
· 1/2 pound monkfish, cut into 1" slices
· 2 tablespoons Italian parsley, freshly chopped

Directions

Rinse *calamari* and cut bodies into 1/2" rings. If tentacles are large, cut in half lengthwise. Shell and devein shrimp. Dry shrimp, sea scallops, and *calamari* over paper towels. Cut octopus into 1" pieces. Lightly salt and pepper.

Heat olive oil in a 6 quart Dutch oven over medium-high heat. Sear shrimp about one minute per side. Remove shrimp to a bowl. Sauté sea scallops about two minutes per side. Remove and add to the bowl with the shrimp. Sauté calamari for a 2-3 minutes. Remove and add to bowl with shrimp and scallops.

Lower heat to medium; add garlic and *peperoncino* and cook for about 30 seconds. Add onions and cook until translucent, about 5 minutes. Add octopus, cover, and cook for 15 minutes. Add red wine and tomato paste and reduce by half. Add tomatoes; cover and simmer over low heat for 35 minutes. Add clams and cook for 5 minutes. Add mussels, fish, shrimp, scallops, and *calamari* and cook for 5 minutes. Add parsley and check seasonings.

Serve in bowls with slices of garlic bread and extra-virgin olive oil.

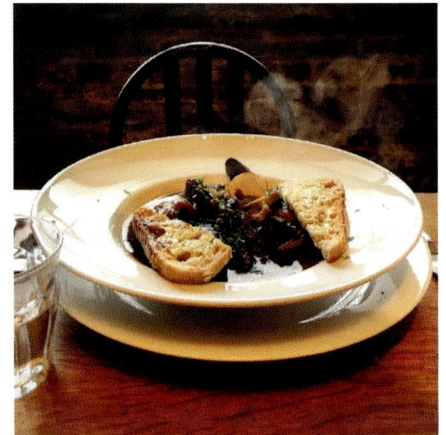

Guazzetto alla Chioggiotta
Venetian Seafood Stew

Alle Testiere is arguably one of the best seafood restaurants in Venice. It's also one of the hardest restaurants in which to get a table; they are booked months in advance. I often go to Venice in October to see the *Biennale Arte* and the *Biennale Architettura*. I make it a point to make my reservation at the restaurant well in advance. This is a small and charming *osteria* with tavern roots; it was once a *bàcaro*. The owners are Luca, who works the front of the house welcoming guests and taking orders with an expressive smile, and Bruno, who is the head chef in the kitchen. Luca's wife makes their mouthwatering desserts. The food and presentation at Alle Testiere are all about freshness and simplicity; they are only open on market days, and the menu changes daily. On my last visit, I ordered their *Guazzetto alla Chioggiotta* as my antipasto. It is a delicious Venetian seafood stew with the unique addition of white wine vinegar.

Wine Pairing

Schiopetto Pinot Bianco,
Friuli Venezia-Giulia

Serves 4

· 4 large shrimp, shelled and deveined
· 4 large head-on *scampi*
· 4 large sea scallops, cut in half cross-wise
· 4 small *calamari* bodies + 4 tentacles
· Salt, to taste
· White pepper, freshly ground to taste
· 2 tablespoon extra-virgin olive oil
· 2 cloves garlic, finely chopped
· 1 large shallot (1/2 cup), finely chopped
· 1 cup fish stock
· 1/2 cup white wine vinegar
· 8 little neck clams
· 12 mussels
· 2 pounds mixed fish, cut into 1" cubes
  (firm fish, such as monkfish and halibut,
  work best)

Directions

Rinse *calamari* and cut bodies into 1/2" rings. If tentacles are large, cut them in half lengthwise. Shell and devein shrimp. Dry shrimp, *scampi*, sea scallops, and *calamari* over paper towels. Lightly salt and pepper.

Heat olive oil in a 6 quart Dutch oven over medium heat. Sauté shrimp and *scampi* in batches, about one minute on each side. Remove shrimp and *scampi* to a bowl. Sauté sea scallops about two minutes per side. Remove and add to bowl with shrimp and *scampi*. Sauté *calamari* for 2-3 minutes. Remove and add to bowl with shrimp, *scampi*, and scallops.

Add garlic and cook for about 30 seconds, until fragrant. And chopped shallots and sauté until soft and translucent, about five minutes. Add fish stock and white wine vinegar and reduce by half. Strain the broth and discard solids. Return broth back to the Dutch oven, add clams and mussels; cover and cook until shells open. Shake the pan from time to time. Mussels will open first. Transfer opened shellfish to the bowl with the shrimp and *scampi*.

Add fish to the pot and simmer for 2-3 minutes, uncovered. Add shrimp, *scampi*, scallops, *calamari*, mussels, and clams and gently simmer for 2-3 minutes to warm. Check seasonings.

Serve in warm bowls with grilled polenta on the side.

Ribollita
Tuscan Bean and Cabbage Soup

Although I love *ribollita*, I rarely order it when I'm in Florence in the summer. This is a hearty, comforting, winter dish made with Tuscan cabbage and white beans. *Ribollita* means re-boiled and was traditionally made with leftover vegetable soup, to which day-old bread and a few new ingredients were added. This is typical of the *cucina povera* style of cooking, by which poor people made the most by using inexpensive ingredients.

Wine Pairing
Selvapiana Chianti Rufina, Toscana

Serves 4-6

- 1 cup dried *cannellini* beans, soaked in water overnight and drained
- 1/4 cup extra-virgin olive oil
- 4 oz Tuscan *prosciutto*, thickly sliced and diced
- 1 medium yellow onion, diced
- 1 leek, rinsed and thinly sliced (white and light green sections only)
- 1 carrot, peeled and diced
- 1 stalk celery, diced
- 2 cloves garlic, finely sliced
- 2 sprigs thyme
- 2 sprigs rosemary
- 2 bay leaves
- 2 tablespoons Italian parsley

- *Peperoncino*, to taste
- l bunch *cavolo nero* (black kale), chopped
- l bunch Swiss chard, stems removed and leaves rolled up and cut into ribbons
- Salt, to taste
- Black pepper, freshly ground to taste
- 4 San Marzano tomatoes from a can, drained and cut into thirds
- 4 cups chicken stock, homemade if possible
- 1 large *Parmigiano* cheese rind
- *Parmigiano Reggiano*, freshly grated

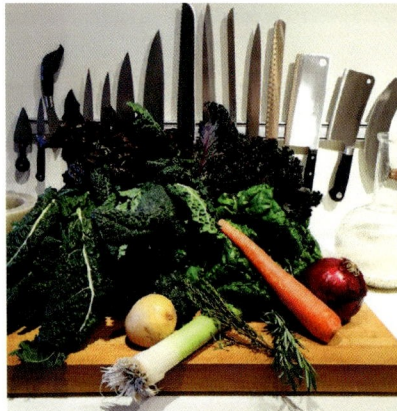

Directions
Place the soaked *cannellini* beans in a medium saucepan and cover with water. Bring to a boil and reduce heat to simmer. Cook beans for 45 minutes until tender.

Heat olive oil in a 6-quart Dutch oven over medium heat. Sauté *prosciutto*, onion, leek, carrot, celery, sliced garlic, thyme, rosemary, bay leaves, parsley, and *peperoncino* until vegetables are soft, about 10 minutes. Add the *cavolo nero* and Swiss chard and continue cooking another 10 minutes. Add salt and pepper to taste along with the tomatoes. Reduce heat to low and cook for another 10 minutes.

Drain *cannellini* beans and add to the large saucepan with the other vegetables. Add the *Parmigiano* cheese rind and chicken stock. Simmer covered for about an hour.

Serve in bowls with slices of garlic bread and a grating of *Parmigiano Reggiano*.

Zuppa di Pesci
Seafood Soup

In the early years of my involvement with Dominican University's Summer Program in Florence, I used to go to Capri every summer. I would take an early morning train to Naples from the Santa Maria Novella railway station. Back then, the trains were compartment cars with strangers sharing food with one another. Once in Naples, it was about an hour's walk to the Porto di Napoli, where I would take a two-hour ferry ride to the beautiful island of Capri. A quick check-in at the hotel, and I could be swimming in the warm, emerald-green water at the Spiaggia di Marina Piccola by mid-afternoon. It was in Capri, off the elegant Piazzetta Umberto I, that I first ordered *zuppa di pesce*, a stew-like mixture of several different kinds of fish and shellfish. This dish evokes my first trip to Capri every time I make it.

Wine Pairing

San Salvatore Falanghina del Beneventano, Campania

Serves 4

· 1 pound *calamari*, 1/2 tubes and 1/2 tentacles
· 1/2 pound shrimp, shelled and deveined
· 1 pound sea scallops, cut in half crosswise
· 4 large head-on *scampi*
· Salt, to taste
· White pepper, freshly ground to taste
· 9 tablespoons extra-virgin olive oil
· 2 cloves garlic, finely sliced
· *Peperoncino*, to taste
· 1 cup dry white wine
· 2 quarts fish stock, homemade if possible
· 12 littleneck clams, rinsed and scrubbed
· 12 mussels, rinsed, scrubbed, and debearded
· 10 ounces cherry tomatoes, cut in half
· 1/2 teaspoon saffron, crushed
· 1 pound monkfish, cut into 1" cubes
· 2 tablespoons Italian parsley, finely chopped
· 2 tablespoons fresh basil, finely chopped

Directions

Rinse *calamari* and cut bodies into 1/2" rings. If tentacles are large, cut them in half lengthwise. Shell and devein shrimp. Dry shrimp, *scampi*, sea scallops, and *calamari* over paper towels. Lightly salt and pepper.

Heat olive oil in a 6 quart Dutch oven over medium heat. Sauté shrimp and *scampi* in batches, about one minute on each side. Remove shrimp and scampi to a bowl. Sauté sea scallops about two minutes per side. Remove and add to bowl with shrimp and *scampi*. Sauté *calamari* for 2-3 minutes. Remove and add to bowl with shrimp, scampi, and scallops.

Add garlic and *peperoncino* and cook for 30 seconds. Add wine and 1/2 cup of stock. Add clams and mussels; cover and cook until shells open. Shake the pan from time to time. Mussels will open first. Transfer opened shellfish to the bowl with the shrimp and *scampi*.

Add remaining stock to the pot with tomatoes and saffron. Check salt and pepper. Simmer uncovered for 20 minutes. Add monkfish to the stock and simmer for 2-3 minutes uncovered. Add shrimp, *scampi*, scallops, *calamari*, mussels, and clams and gently simmer for 2-3 minutes to warm. Check seasonings; add basil and parsley.

Serve in warm bowls with slices of garlic bread.

SECONDI—PESCE

Baccalà alla Vicentina
Codfish Vicenza-Style

I'm not a big fan of fresh cod; it's too mild and boring for my taste. It also falls apart easily and, in a sauce, it practically disappears. Salt cod, on the other hand, is a whole different animal. It's flavorful and firmer in texture and lends itself to dozens of cooking options. The first time I ate *baccalà alla vicentina* was over twenty years ago in Vicenza, the city of its origin. I was on a weekend trip from Florence with my colleague, Anthony Gully, and his wife, Anne. We went to see the magnificent buildings by the Renaissance architect, Andrea Palladio. The day we arrived, we had lunch at Al Pestello, a first-class restaurant that's been around since 1910. That lunch was my introduction to this delicious and complex dish. *Baccalà alla vicentina* is savory, yet sweet because of the caramelized onions and milk. It has wine; it has anchovies; it even has cheese. It was a meal I'll never forget and a dish I've had many times since. After lunch, we took in Palladio's harmonious palaces, churches, and his classically inspired *Teatro Olimpico*. Our plan for our second day included renting bicycles from our hotel to visit Palladio's villas in the surrounding countryside, and having a picnic. That morning we went to the famous Gastronomia Il Ceppo to purchase the fixings for our lunch. It was a memorable feast, with assorted cured meats (including horse prosciutto), cheese, *vitello tonnato* (veal with a tuna-caper sauce), bread, wine, and, yes, more *baccalà alla vicentina*, which, as it turns out, is quite delicious served at room temperature.

Wine Pairing
Montecariano Madonna, Veneto

Serves 4-6
· 2 pounds salt cod (boneless and skinless)
· 2 tablespoons unsalted butter
· 1 yellow onion, finely minced
· 4 garlic cloves, finely sliced
· 6 anchovy fillets, chopped
· 1 tablespoon Italian parsley, finely chopped
· 5 tablespoons extra-virgin olive oil
· 1/2 cup unbleached all-purpose flour
· 1 teaspoon salt
· 1 teaspoon white pepper, freshly ground
· 1/2 cup *Parmigiano Reggiano*, freshly grated
· 1 cup dry white wine
· 1 1/2 cups milk

Directions
Soak the salt cod in cold water in the refrigerator for 2 days, changing water twice a day.

Poach cod fillets for two minutes in boiling water. Drain and allow to dry; cut into 3" square pieces.

In a 14" frying pan, melt the butter and sauté garlic and anchovies over low heat until fragrant. Add onions and parsley and continue to sauté until onions are slightly browned. Remove garlic-anchovy-onion-parsley mixture and set aside.

Add olive oil to pan and heat to medium-high.

Mix flour with salt and pepper on a large plate. Lightly dredge the cod pieces and fry for about 10 minutes until brown, flipping once after five minutes. Add grated *Parmigiano*, onion mixture, and wine over medium heat until alcohol evaporates. Add milk and reduce to simmer. Cover frying pan and simmer 2-3 hours over very low heat. Check fish periodically with a spatula to make sure it's not sticking to the pan. If needed, add 2-3 tablespoons of milk to loosen fish. Serve over white or yellow *polenta*.

Baccalà Fritto alla Romana
Fried Salt Cod Roman Style

I'm always intrigued when I see a long line of locals waiting outside a restaurant for a table, especially when I can see that the interior of the establishment is lit by blinding white florescent lighting. I'm even more intrigued when the sign above the door says FILLETE BACCALÀ. This is Dar Filettaro a Santa Barbara. It's a small traditional Roman *trattoria* on the ancient Piazza Santa Barbara, a mere 2-minute walk from the Campo de' Fiori in central Rome. People line up here for one thing – fried salt cod or *baccalà fritto alla romana*. This is their specialty, and they do it very well. Their fillets of *baccalà* are thick and meaty, perfectly battered, and fried until crunchy and golden. In the winter months, the *contorno* or side-dish of choice is *puntarelle alla romana* (a variant of chicory) served with a garlic anchovy vinaigrette. Simple ingredients, simply prepared. I understand that their batter recipe is a closely guarded secret. I've decided that less is best. Below is my attempt to recreate their version of salt cod heaven.

Wine Pairing

Fantini Farnese Cocacciola Cuvee, Abruzzo

Serves 2-4

· 1 pound salt cod
· 1 cup all-purpose flour
· 1 cup cold premium lager beer, such as Nastro Azzuro
· 16 oz sunflower or safflower oil (both have high smoke points)
· Sea salt, to taste
· Black pepper, freshly ground to taste
· 1 tablespoon Italian parsley, finely minced

Directions

Soak the salt cod in cold water and place in the refrigerator for 2-3 days, changing water 2-3 times a day. Taste the cod before you are ready to cook it. It should no longer be overly salty.

Measure out flour in a large bowl, add cold beer a little at a time, and whisk thoroughly. The batter should coat a spoon. You may need to add more beer if the batter is too thick.

Cut cod into strips 4"- 5" long and dry well with paper towels. Heat oil to 375 degrees Fahrenheit in a 4-quart sauce pot. The high sides will reduce spattering. Use a deep fry thermometer to monitor the heat.

Dip cod strips in batter to coat and fry in small batches (2-3 pieces at a time). You don't want to crowd the pot. Fry 2 minutes per side until golden. Keep a close eye on heat fluctuations and adjust burner accordingly. Do not let oil cool down below 350 degrees Fahrenheit.

Remove cod from the oil with a slotted skimmer or kitchen spider and place on paper towels or the inside of a brown paper bag cut to the dimensions of your plate to drain. Sprinkle salt and freshly ground black pepper to taste, along with parsley, and serve immediately with lemon wedges and *puntarelle alla romana*.

Branzino al Finocchio e Patate
Sea Bass with Fennel and Potatoes

I like my fish to look like fish. I want to see and, later, nibble on the head, skin, tail, and fins. I always insist on de-boning my own fish in restaurants. One, because I look like a badass doing it, and, two, why allow the waiter to cart away those tasty fish cheeks. Although I occasionally like a grilled salmon or swordfish steak, I prefer smaller delicate whitefish like *orata*, *branzino*, and red snapper; all are interchangeable in the following recipe. I like to serve one whole fish for each of my guests.

Wine Pairing

Punta Crena Lumassina Bianco Colline Savonesi, Liguria

Serves 2

· 2 small *branzini*, gutted and scaled with gills removed
· 2 medium fennel bulbs (approximately 12 oz)
· 12 oz fingerling potatoes
· 2 garlic cloves, thinly sliced
· 9 tablespoons extra-virgin olive oil
· Salt, to taste
· White pepper, freshly ground to taste
· 4 sprigs of rosemary
· 10 sprigs thyme
· 2 tablespoon fennel seeds, toasted

Directions

Preheat oven to 400 degrees Fahrenheit.

Cut stalks and fronds off the fennel bulbs and reserve. Trim 1/4" off the bottom of the fennel bulbs and slice fennel bulbs lengthwise into 1" wedges. You don't need to core the bulb; it's edible. Cut fingerling potatoes in half lengthwise. Place potatoes and fennel slices in a 13" x 18" sheet pan lined with parchment paper. Add 3 tablespoons of olive oil and mix to coat thoroughly. Add salt and pepper to taste.

Roast vegetables on a middle shelf in the oven until browned, about 45 minutes. Check to make sure the fennel does not burn. Remove fennel if it looks like its browning too fast. When vegetables are done, remove sheet pan from oven and set on top of the stove.

Preheat oven to broil.

Place fish on a roasting pan and score both sides of the fish with 5-6 diagonal cuts. Stuff fish with a few fennel stalks, sliced garlic, rosemary, and thyme. Add salt and pepper inside the cavity of the fish and on the skin. Brush each fish with 2 tablespoons of olive oil inside and out. Loosely cover tail with tin foil.

Place fish on middle shelf about 8" from broiler. Broil for 6 minutes. Turn oven off and lower fish to bottom shelf for an additional 4-5 minutes. Place fennel and potatoes back in the oven for 4-5 minutes to reheat while fish finishes cooking. Fish is done when a metal skewer inserted into the fish is warm on the lips.

While fish is cooking, toast fennel seeds in a small frying pan over medium heat until fragrant; set aside. Serve fish with roasted vegetables and garnish with toasted fennel seeds and fennel fronds.

Calamari in Zimino
Squid Braised with Chard

This is an interesting Tuscan and Ligurian dish that can have several variations. At its core, there is *calamari* or cuttlefish braised with greens. The greens can be chard or spinach or a combination of the two. *Calamari in Zimino* can be served as a soup, a thick stew, or a pasta sauce. The first time I ordered it in Florence was at the Trattoria Borgo Antico overlooking Brunelleschi's Basilica di Santo Spirito. The version I ate there was more like a thick stew with relatively little sauce. On another occasion at La Beppa Fioraia, it was served with *rigatoni*. You'll find this recipe inexpensive, easy to make, and very healthy.

Wine Pairing

Fattoria Le Pupille Poggio Argentato, Toscana

Serves 4-6

· 2 pounds Swiss Chard, large stems removed
· 2 tablespoons extra virgin olive oil
· 1 red onion, finely chopped
· 1 stalk celery, finely chopped
· 2 garlic cloves, finely chopped
· 2-3 sprigs of Italian parsley, finely chopped
· Salt, to taste
· White pepper, freshly ground to taste
· 2 pounds *calamari* (tubes and tentacles)
· 1 tablespoon doppio concentrato di pomodoro (double-concentrated tomato paste)
· *Peperoncino*, to taste
· 1/2 cup dry white wine

Directions

Bring 8 quarts of water to boil in a large pot. Roughly chop up the chard and add to the boiling water for 1 minute to blanch. Drain in a colander under cold running water. When the chard is cold, squeeze out the water with your hands and set aside.

Heat oil in a large Dutch oven over medium-high heat. Add the chopped onion, celery, garlic, parsley, salt, and pepper. Sauté until vegetables are soft; this is your *soffritto*.

Cut the *calamari* bodies into 1/2" rings and cut the tentacles in half. Add the *calamari* to the vegetables and cook for five minutes. Add tomato paste, *peperoncino*, and wine; continue cooking another five minutes. Add the chard to the *calamari* and vegetables; mix, cover, and simmer over low heat for 20 minutes. Serve hot in bowls with crusty bread for dipping into the sauce.

Coda di Rospo alla Griglia
Grilled Monkfish

Many years ago, during my first summer teaching in Italy, I took a weekend trip from Florence to see the Venice Biennale. It was July and very hot and humid. Nevertheless, I immediately fell in love with the city. I was fascinated by the soft light, the reflections on the water, the sounds of the *vaporetti*, the art, and the food. I have returned to the city every year since. That summer I tasted *coda di rospo* for the first time at the Trattoria Alla Rivetta. This bustling *trattoria* was and still is a very popular restaurant near San Marco. It's always packed with tourists, locals, and gondoliers, with everyone sharing tables and eating side by side. I haven't eaten there in years, but their *coda di rospo* served on the bone was a memorable experience. It was grilled whole with its cartiligenous vertebrae until golden brown. Monkfish don't have many bones; their skeleton is made from cartilage, which, I remember, surprised me as I was able to gnaw through most of it. I've had *coda di rospo* in Venice many times since, usually prepared very simply, grilled with olive oil and lemon. The following recipe is my version of this delicious, ugly fish.

Wine Pairing
Scarbolo "My Time," Friuli Venezia-Giulia

Serves 2
· 1 pound monkfish fillet
· 2 tablespoon extra-virgin olive oil
· 2 tablespoon dry white wine
· 2 tablespoons fresh lemon juice
· 2 garlic cloves
· 2 tablespoons Italian parsley, finely chopped
· 1/4 teaspoon Maldon smoked salt
· 1/4 teaspoon white pepper, freshly ground
· 1 tablespoon salted capers (rinsed)

Directions
Preheat oven to broil.

Carefully remove all traces of the silver skin and blood lines from the fish fillet. Remaining silver skin will shrink when cooked and will tighten the fillet into an irregular shape. Mix olive oil, wine, lemon juice, garlic, salt, and pepper in a bowl and pour into a large zip lock plastic bag. Add monkfish to bag and marinate for 30-45 minutes.

Once the fish has marinated and the oven has pre-heated, place fish fillet with the more attractive side facing up on the broiling pan insert. Pour marinade over fish.

Broil for approximately 10 minutes on top shelf of the oven, approximately 6" from broiler, until browned. To check for doneness, insert a thin metal skewer in the thickest part of the fillet; it should penetrate easily and be warm when taken out. If there are spots that are not browned, drizzle a little more olive oil and continue broiling for another minute or two.

Serve topped with capers, a healthy drizzle of good extra-virgin olive oil, smoked salt, and several lemon wedges. Slice on an angle with a very sharp knife.

Fritto Misto di Mare
Mixed Fried Seafood

Nothing evokes summer, beach life, and the sea as much as *fritto misto di mare*. Italians love it, and so do I. All along the almost five-thousand miles of Italian coastline, the scent of fried seafood permeates the air, beginning around noon every day during the summer months. *Fritto misto* is consistently good because the seafood is fresh, and it's prepared simply with no heavy batter, no cornmeal, no eggs – just flour and hot oil. Over the past 25 years I've spent most of my summers in Italy. *Fritto misto* has always been a part of those summer experiences. So much so that I usually have a hard time ordering anything else on the menu at lunchtime. It's that intoxicating. When I'm teaching in Florence, I usually spend at least one day a week on the beach at Viareggio on the Tuscan coast. My favorite beach club is the Bagno Tres Stelle, and one of my favorite restaurants in town is the Ristorante Sa Playa next door. There, I can have my *fritto misto* for lunch with a half-liter of white wine, sitting outdoors on the boulevard before heading back to my beach bed for an afternoon siesta – *La dolce vita*.

Wine Pairing
Bibi Graetz Casamatta Bianco, Toscana

Serves 2-4
· 1/2 pound *calamari* (1/2 tubes and 1/2 tentacles), rinsed
· 1/2 pound shrimp, shelled and deveined, tail left on
· 1/2 pound small octopus, eyes, head and beak removed
· 1 lemon
· 6 sprigs rosemary
· 1 quart sunflower or safflower oil (both have high smoke points)
· 2 cups unbleached all-purpose flour
· 1 teaspoon salt
· 1 teaspoon white pepper, freshly ground
· 1/2 teaspoon cayenne pepper (optional)

The seafood ingredients in this recipe can be altered to include fresh scallops (sliced in half crosswise), small sardines or smelt, shelled mussels, etc. You can also add another pound of seafood without changing the flour and oil measurements. Just make sure not to fry more than a half pound of seafood at a time. You don't want the oil to cool down, and you don't want the seafood to stick together.

Directions
Slice the *calamari* tubes into ½ rings; keep tentacles whole and set on paper towels to dry along with shrimp. Cut octopus tentacles into 3″ segments and set on paper towels to dry.

Cut half of a lemon into 1/4 slices and the other half into six wedges.

Heat oil in a 4-quart pot to 375 degrees Fahrenheit. (Olive oil will burn at this temperature.) Use a deep-frying thermometer with a range of 100-400 degrees Fahrenheit.

Mix flour, salt, and pepper in a medium bowl. Set a larger bowl with a kitchen strainer next to the hot oil. Divide mixed seafood into 3-4 batches.

Dredge seafood, lemon slices, and rosemary in the flour; shake in strainer over large bowl to remove excess flour and carefully place into the hot oil with a kitchen spider. Cook for approximately 3 minutes until golden. Octopus may take a minute or two longer, so you may wish to put it in the oil first. Add lemon slices and rosemary sprigs into the oil last and cook for 1 minute.

Remove seafood, lemon, and rosemary with a kitchen spider and drain on a rack placed in a sheet pan; salt and serve immediately with fresh lemon wedges. *Fritto misto* should be eaten as soon as it's out of the oil, so invite your friends and family into the kitchen to use their fingers to eat off the cooling rack while you fry up another batch.

Orata con Patate e Olive
Seabream with Potatoes and Olives

I love the creamy delicate flavor of new potatoes. Whenever I see fingerlings or tiny round potatoes at the farmers' market, I immediately begin thinking about building a meal around them. This dish was inspired by many memorable lunches in Cinque Terre. I'm using *orata* here, but you could easy substitute other mild whitefish, such as *branzino* or red snapper. Many recipes call for this trio of fish, potatoes, and olives to be baked. I prefer a little char on my fish skin, so I like to broil it.

Wine Pairing

Durin Pigato, Liguria

Serves 2

· 2 small *orate*, gutted and scaled with gills removed
· 1 pound fingerling potatoes or small round potatoes
· 1/2 pound black *Gaeta* or *Niçoise* olives, un-pitted
· 2 garlic cloves, thinly sliced
· 6-8 tablespoons extra-virgin olive oil
· Salt, to taste
· White pepper, freshly ground to taste
· 4 sprigs rosemary
· 10 sprigs thyme
· 1/2 lemon, thinly sliced

Directions

Preheat oven to 425 degrees Fahrenheit.

Using a very sharp knife, cut 5-6 diagonal cuts on each side of the fish. Stuff fish cavity with rosemary, thyme, lemon, garlic, and salt and pepper and drizzle with olive oil. Salt and pepper the outside of the fish and brush an additional tablespoon of olive oil on each fish. Place on a broiler pan; loosely cover tail with tin foil; set aside.

If using fingerling potatoes, cut them in half lengthwise. If using tiny round potatoes, 1" small, leave whole. Place potatoes in a bowl; add 2 tablespoons of olive oil, a good amount of salt and pepper to taste; toss to coat. Place on 13"x18" sheet pan lined with parchment paper.

Place sheet pan on middle shelf of pre-heated oven and bake until brown (approximately 30 minutes). Shake pan periodically. When done, remove from oven and place on stove.

Preheat oven to broil.

Place fish on middle shelf, about 8" from broiler. Broil for 6 minutes. Turn oven off and lower fish to bottom shelf for an additional 4-5 minutes. Place potatoes and black olives back in the oven for 4-5 minutes to reheat while fish finishes cooking. Fish is done when a metal skewer inserted into the fish is warm on the lips. Serve fish with potatoes and olives. Remind guests that the olives are un-pitted.

Polpo alla Griglia
Grilled Octopus

One of my favorite things to do in Bari is to go to the Sunday fish market on the Mola San Nicola. There you will see for sale mountains of raw mussels, clams, prawns, *calamari*, sea urchins, oysters, and baby octopuses no bigger than your thumb an forefinger. Much of them are eaten raw right on the pier next to the colorful fishing boats. The Barese love *crudo* or raw seafood. Several enterprising fishermen lay out plastic plates for 5 euros, each filled with *crudo* that must be washed down with an obligatory bottle of Peroni beer available at the Bar El Chiringuito on the pier. One of the more entertaining sights is to watch the octopus fishermen in their orange and yellow overalls tenderize their larger eight-legged catch by slapping them on the concrete pavement and whacking them repeatedly with large flat wooden paddles, all the while yelling something in Barese dialect that is impenetrably difficult to understand. Bari, and Puglia in general, has lots of sandwich shops and stands specializing in octopus sandwiches. On the southern edge of the historic center, Mastro Ciccio makes delicious octopus sandwiches with mozzarella, sun-dried tomatoes, and arugula. If you get the chance, try one on a black bun, made with squid ink. Another block into the old section you'll find La Tana del Polpo, which not only serves very good meals in the restaurant itself but also sells fried octopus sandwiches with plastic cups of white wine as street food. Pescobar has a shop on the Lungomare and also at the beach at Torre Quetta, two miles southeast of Bari. It sells a minimal but delicious octopus sandwich. The following recipe calls for cooking octopus *sous-vide* and then broiling it in the oven to get a little char on the suction cups. If you have an outdoor grill, that's even better.

Wine Pairing

Masseria Li Veli Verdeca "Askos," Puglia

Makes 2 sandwiches

· 2 large tentacles (about 1/2 pounds each) or
  2 medium-sized whole octopuses
· 2-3 tablespoons extra-virgin olive oil
· 4 oz fresh mozzarella, sliced
· 4 sun-dried tomatoes
· 1/2 cup baby arugula
· Maldon smoked sea salt, to taste
· 2 crusty round bread rolls or large baguette

Directions

Heat sous-vide bath to 180 degrees Fahrenheit.

Meanwhile, blanch octopus in rapidly boiling water for 5-10 minutes until tentacles curl up. Immediately place into an ice bath. Once the octopus has cooled, carefully remove from ice bath and dry thoroughly. Take care not to tear the purple skin. Separate large tentacles; place into two Foodsaver bags and vacuum seal. If using smaller octopuses, remove the center beak and cut off the head just below the eyes. You can cook the smaller octopuses whole.

Place octopus in the *sous-vide* bath and cook for 4 hours. Once cooked, place the Foodsaver bags containing the octopus in another ice water bath.

Preheat oven to broil.

Remove octopus from the Foodsaver bags, dry well, and place on a broiling pan. Brush with olive oil and salt lightly. Place broiling pan on the top shelf about 6" from broiler. Broil for about 8 minutes. The smaller octopuses may take less time; check on them after 5-6 minutes. I like a little char on the tentacles, but you don't want to carbonize them.

To assemble sandwich: generously brush both sides of the bread rolls with olive oil add 2 oz of sliced mozzarella, 1/4 cup of arugula, octopus, and 2 sundried tomatoes. Use a wooden skewer to hold everything together. Depending on how thick the large tentacles are, you may wish to cut them in half vertically.

Rombo al Forno con Patate, Pomodorini, Olive e Capperi
Baked Turbot with Potatoes, Cherry Tomatoes, Olives and Capers

I first had r*ombo al forno* at the Ristorante La Battigia in Bari. La Battigia, which means shoreline in Italian, is a wonderful seafood restaurant located across the street from the waterfront and the fish market on the Molo S. Nicolo. The fish is always super fresh and beautifully displayed in the main dining room, like a still life painting by Frans Snyders. A few years ago I ate lunch there every day for two months. Each day, the waiter would accompany me to the display case and discuss different preparations for my choice of fish. One day, I was intrigued by a large flatfish with both eyes on the same side of its head. That fish was one of the most memorable seafood experiences I've ever had. I had the *rombo* baked whole with thin slices of potatoes and cherry tomatoes. Later that year in December, I rented an apartment for three weeks in the Prati neighborhood north of the Vatican. I was very excited to find a fresh whole *rombo* at the *pescheria* (fish market) in the Mercato Vittoria around the corner from my apartment. I rushed home with my find and immediately began searching the internet for recipes.

Wine Pairing

Tormaresca Calafuria Rosato, Puglia

Serves 2

· 2 pounds whole turbot (head and skin on, rinsed)
· 8 oz small wax potatoes, cut into 1/2" rounds
· 8 oz fresh cherry tomatoes, cut in half
· 3/4 cup dry white wine
· 3/4 cup *Gaeta* or *Niçoise* olives, un-pitted
· 5-6 whole garlic cloves (in their paper skin)
· 2 tablespoons extra-virgin olive oil
· Salt, to taste
· White pepper, freshly ground to taste
· 1 1/2 tablespoons salted capers, rinsed
· 4-5 sprigs rosemary
· 4-5 sprigs Italian parsley
· 3-4 fresh bay leaves

Directions

Preheat oven to 350 degrees Fahrenheit.

Line a baking sheet pan with parchment paper. Place fish on bed of rosemary, bay leaves, and parsley. Add salt and freshly ground pepper to taste. Add potatoes, tomatoes, olives, garlic, and capers around and on top of the fish. Brush fish and vegetables with olive oil; pour wine over fish.

Cook on middle shelf with convection fan (if you have one) for approximately 45 min. Check on fish after 20 minutes. Add a little water if liquid is evaporating. Turn pan around and continue cooking.

Serve fish on a large platter with potatoes, tomatoes, olives, capers, and rosemary. Remind guests that the olives are un-pitted.

SECONDI—POLLAME

Anatra in Porchetta Infinocchiata
Duck in the Manner of Porchetta

I love going to the monthly antique fair in Arezzo, which takes place on the first Sunday of every month. It's very popular, and it's not uncommon to bump into someone you know. My routine has not changed much over the last twenty-five years. I arrive mid-morning by train from Florence; I walk through the fair and the main square scouting out things to buy that I don't really need; I visit Piero della Francesca in the church of San Francesco; I have a Negroni at the Café Paris; and then I have lunch at one of my favorite restaurants in Tuscany, the Trattoria Il Saraceno, where I always reserve one of the small tables by the open window. This cozy little restaurant has been serving up tasty Tuscan fare, like wild boar, hare, rabbit, and tripe since 1946. The last time I ate there, I ordered their moist and flavorful roast duck in porchetta. For me, dessert at Il Saraceno is always a plate of fresh and aged *pecorino toscano* served with local honey followed by a cup of *espresso* and a glass of aged *grappa*. It's really a perfect way to spend a Sunday. I've recreated their dish with the same herbs and spices that I use for my *porchettina*.

Wine Pairing

Ornellaia Le Volte dell'Ornellaia, Toscana

Serves 2-4

· 1 whole duck (approximately 5 pounds), reserve neck, liver, heart, and kidneys
· 1/3 cup fennel fronds, chopped
· 1/3 cup rosemary leaves, chopped
· 12 sage leaves, chopped
· 3 cloves garlic, thinly sliced
· Grated zest from 1 lemon
· 1 teaspoon kosher salt
· 1/2 teaspoon freshly ground black pepper
· 1/2 tablespoon fennel seeds
· 1/2 teaspoon *peperoncino*
· 1/2 teaspoon black pepper, freshly ground
· 2 tablespoons extra-virgin olive oil
· 1 large fennel bulb, chopped

Directions

Add fennel fronds, rosemary, sage, garlic, lemon zest, salt, fennel seeds, *peperoncino*, black pepper, and olive oil to a food processor and pulse several times.

For the stuffing, roughly chop fennel bulb, duck liver, heart and kidneys. Add half of the spice and herb mixture; mix and refrigerate.

Prick the skin of the duck on all sides with a knife. This will release the duck fat when it's roasting. Take care not to cut into the meat. Cut excess fat flaps but leave enough to tie up and close both ends of the duck. Rub remaining spice and herb mixture all over the duck, inside and out. Place uncovered duck on a cooking rack over a roasting pan. Place in the refrigerator overnight to dry out. Add neck to the bottom of the pan.

Chop fat into small pieces and render over low heat until crispy. These cracklings are great sprinkled over a salad.

The next day, preheat oven to 450 degrees Fahrenheit

Place chopped fennel-liver mixture in the cavity of the duck and truss duck. Cook duck, breast side down, for 30 minutes. Reduce heat to 350 degrees; turn duck over so that the breast faces up and continue cooking for another 30 minutes. After 1 hour cover wing tips with tin foil and continue cooking until legs are loose and the internal temperature hits 160 degrees.

When done place duck on cutting board breast side down and cover loosely with tin foil. Let duck rest for 15 minutes to allow juices to redistribute. Carve like a chicken; serve with roast potatoes and fennel stuffing.

Fagiano Arrosto
Roast Pheasant

I love game birds. Unfortunately, many people are unsure how to cook them. The truth is, they're really not much different from chickens; perhaps a little tougher and gamier, but I like that. I find the taste of game birds to be much more flavorful than domestic chickens. Pheasants will remain moist if they are brined before roasting and covered with *pancetta* before being placed in the oven. Add some fingerling potatoes, tossed with olive oil and salt, under the roasting rack, and some *funghi trifolati* (sautéed mushrooms) for a complete Umbrian meal.

Here at home, I buy the *pancetta pepata* made by the Salumeria Biellese in New York City. They make a delicious, air-dried, unrolled *pancetta*, seasoned with fresh rosemary and cracked pepper.

Wine Pairing
Lungarotti Rubesco Sangiovese Colorino, Toscana

Serves 2-4
· 2 1/2 pound pheasant
· 4 quarts water
· 1 cup kosher salt
· 1/4 cup sugar
· 4 bay leaves
· 2 tablespoons juniper berries
· Salt, to taste
· Black pepper, freshly ground to taste
· *Pancetta pepata*, thinly sliced to cover bird
· 2 sprigs fresh rosemary
· 2 sprigs fresh thyme
· 2 stems fresh sage leaves
· 1 tablespoon extra-virgin olive oil

Directions
To brine the bird, fill a large stock pot with water, kosher salt, sugar, bay leaves and juniper berries. Bring water to a boil to dissolve salt and sugar; let cool. Place the bird in the water, cover and refrigerate for 6-8 hours. Remove bird from the brine and dry well with paper towels. Season the bird inside and out with salt and pepper. Place breast side up in a roasting pan fitted with a rack and refrigerate uncovered overnight for up to 12 hours. This step dries out the skin, but not the meat, so the bird browns better.

Preheat oven to 450 degrees Fahrenheit. Remove bird from the refrigerator 30 minutes before roasting.

Bundle the herbs, tie with kitchen twine, and place inside the cavity of the bird. Truss the legs with kitchen twine and return the bird breast side up to the roasting pan with a rack. The rack will allow air to circulate under the bird and will help the underside of the bird to brown.

Rub olive oil all over the outside of the bird and cover with strips of *pancetta*. Roast for 45 minutes; then baste with the pan juices. Continue roasting for another 10-20 minutes until a meat thermometer inserted into the thickest part of the thigh reads 160 degrees; legs should be loose and juices should be clear.

Let the bird rest for ten minutes before carving. Serve with roast potatoes and *funghi trifolati*.

Piccione Arrosto
Roast Squab

Lately, I've become obsessed with roasting small game birds. They remind me of the hills of Tuscany, Umbria, and Sardegna. There's something romantic and mystical about these small birds. I think of long medieval banquette tables with everyone eating with their hands; there really is no other way to eat these birds. Of course, they also remind me of Chardin's kitchen still life paintings, in which they share the scene with hand-forged copper pots and an occasional wild rabbit. Although cooking small birds over an open fire is ideal, I don't have a grill, so I roast my birds in the oven. There are lots of recipes involving grapes, pomegranate seeds, and sausage stuffing. I prefer simplicity; I want the flavor of the birds to dominate. Feel free to substitute any number of small game birds, such as partridge and quail, for the squab in this recipe.

Wine Pairing

Antonelli Montelfalco Rosso, Umbria

Serves 2

· 2 squabs
· Salt, to taste
· Black pepper, freshly ground to taste
· 2 sprigs fresh rosemary
· 2 stems fresh sage leaves
· *Pancetta pepata* (Salumeria Biellese), thinly sliced to cover bird
· 1 tablespoon extra-virgin olive oil

Directions

If your squabs have not been eviscerated, you will need to do that (not one of my favorite tasks). Cut off the head and neck as close to the body as possible. Then make a cut on the opposite end; reach in and remove the heart, lungs, kidneys, gizzard, entrails – everything. It's best to do this in the sink. When done, rinse birds inside and out with cold water until no blood remains. Dry birds with paper towels. Wash knife, sink, hands, and countertop with soap and water.

Preheat oven to 400 degrees Fahrenheit. If you have a convection fan, turn it on.

Salt and pepper the birds and place the herbs inside the cavity of the birds. Rub olive oil all over the outside of the bird and cover with strips of *pancetta* secured with a couple of toothpicks. Place the birds, breast side up, in the bottom of a small sheet pan. Roast for approximately 15 minutes until a meat thermometer inserted into the breast reads 125-130 degrees. Squab should be served slightly underdone to retain moistness

Let the birds rest for five minutes before carving. Serve with *funghi trifolati* (sautéed mushrooms).

Pollo alla Cacciatora
Chicken Hunter's Style

This chicken dish is classic Italian comfort food. I've substituted bone-in, skinless chicken thighs in place of a whole chicken. I prefer their taste to breast meat and using all thighs ensures that the meat will cook evenly. Bone-in thighs look and cook better than boneless thighs. Furthermore, I think chicken skin only belongs on crispy, roasted chicken. You could, if you wish, substitute a whole rabbit in this recipe. I add some *guanciale*, which gives the dish a little earthier flavor. Feel free to leave it out or use *pancetta* instead. Some recipes call for the addition of red peppers; I leave them out in this version. The use of red or white wine is also an option; I prefer white. This dish tastes even better the next day and is great at room temperature at a picnic or on a day at the beach.

Wine Pairing
Fattoria Le Pupille Morellino di Scansano, Toscana

Serves 4
· 3 oz dried *porcini* mushrooms
· 1 cup chicken stock
· 3 pounds chicken thighs, bone-in, skinless
· Salt, to taste
· Black pepper, freshly ground to taste
· 1/4 cup olive oil
· 3 oz *guanciale*, cut into lardons
· 3 cloves of garlic, finely minced
· 2 sprigs rosemary leaves, minced
· 1 teaspoon thyme, minced
· 1 bay leaf
· *Peperoncino*, to taste
· 1/2 carrot, peeled and finely chopped
· 1 large yellow onion, finely chopped
· 1 stalk celery, finely chopped
· 1 cup dry white wine
· 14 oz can of San Marzano tomatoes, crushed
· 1/2 cup black *Gaeta* or *Niçoise* olives, un-pitted
· 1/4 cup capers, drained
· 1 tablespoon Italian parsley, finely chopped

Directions
Soak the porcini mushrooms in 1 cup of warm chicken stock until softened, about 30 minutes. Strain liquid through a sieve and reserve.

Dry chicken well and season with salt and freshly ground black pepper.

Heat oil in a large Dutch oven over medium-high heat. Brown chicken in batches, about 10-12 minutes. Be careful not to crowd the pot. Remove chicken to a plate and set aside.

Add *guanciale* and cook over low heat until fat is rendered and it becomes crispy. Add garlic, rosemary leaves, thyme, bay leaf, *peperoncino*, carrot, onion, and celery to the pot and cook over medium-low heat until onions are translucent, about 10 minutes.

Add wine; increase heat to medium and reduce by half, about 5 minutes. Return chicken to pot with juices, crushed tomatoes, *porcini* mushrooms, and the strained chicken stock used to soak the mushrooms. Bring to a low simmer and cook covered for 30 minutes. Stir in olives and capers immediately before serving.

Serve family style on a large platter; garnish with freshly chopped parsley. Remind guests that the olives are un-pitted.

Pollo alla Puttanesca
Chicken alla Puttanesca

Among the first cookbooks I purchased after graduate school were the *Silver Palette Cookbook* and the *Silver Palette Good Times Cookbook*, first published in the early 1980s. The authors, Julee Rosso and Sheila Lukins, made cooking fun. Their inspirational recipes reflected the seasons and holidays. Their recipes were exotic at the time, and the combination of herbs and spices in their recipes was often assertive and pungent. This is my adaptation of their classic *Chicken alla Puttanesca*.

Wine Pairing

Valentina Passalacqua Terra Sasso, Puglia

Serves 4

· 3 pounds chicken thighs, bone-in, skinless
· Salt, to taste
· Black pepper, freshly ground to taste
· 1/4 cup olive oil
· 12 cloves of garlic, finely minced
· 2 teaspoons rosemary leaves, minced
· 1 teaspoon thyme, minced
· 1 bay leaf
· *Peperoncino*, to taste
· 1 medium yellow onion, finely chopped
· 1 tablespoon red wine vinegar
· 28 oz canned *pomodorini* (cherry tomatoes), crushed
· 1/4 cup sun-dried tomatoes, chopped
· 2 oz anchovies, drained
· 1/2 cup black *gaeta or niçoise* olives, un-pitted
· 1/4 cup capers, drained
· 1/4 cup fresh basil, roughly chopped

Directions

Dry chicken well and season with salt and freshly ground black pepper.

Heat oil in a large Dutch oven over medium-high heat. Brown chicken in batches, about 10-12 minutes. Be careful not to crowd the pot. Remove chicken to a plate and set aside.

Add garlic, rosemary, thyme, bay leaf, *peperoncino*, and onions to the pot and cook over medium-low heat until onions are translucent, about 10 minutes.

Return chicken to pot with juices; add red wine vinegar, *pomodorini*, sun-dried tomatoes, and anchovies. Bring to a low simmer and cook covered for 30 minutes. Stir in olives and capers immediately before serving. Garnish with chopped basil.

Pollo Arrosto Intero
Whole Roast Chicken

Pollo allo spiedo or spit-roasted chicken, along with other roasted meats, can be found in rosticcerie all over Florence. Sometimes these shops are simple takeaway places with no apparent name, such as the *rosticceria* on the Via Cavour near San Marco. Sometimes, a *rosticceria* might also serve pizza from a wood-burning oven, as does La Mangiatoia on the Piazza San Felice near the Palazzo Pitti. One of my favorites, however, has always been La Spada on the Via Spada. In recent years, this old school Tuscan eatery has added additional tables and changed its name to Ristorante-Rosticceria. They can, however, still be counted on to roast beautiful, delicious chicken on the spit. Unfortunately, most of us don't have a spit; here's a recipe that will yield a crispy, golden brown, Sunday afternoon chicken every time. Add some fingerling potatoes to the pan under the chicken, and you'll have a complete meal.

Wine Pairing

Pieri Rosso di Montalcino, Toscana

Serves 2-4

· 3-4 pound organic free-range chicken, air dried and trimmed of excess fat
· 1 tablespoon kosher salt
· 2 teaspoons black pepper, freshly ground
· 2 sprigs fresh rosemary
· 2 sprigs fresh thyme
· 2 stems fresh sage leaves
· 1 tablespoon extra-virgin olive oil
· Truffle salt, to taste

Directions

Season the chicken inside and out with salt and pepper. Place breast side up in a roasting pan fitted with a rack and refrigerate uncovered overnight for up to 12 hours. This step dries out the skin so the bird browns better.

Preheat oven to 450 degrees Fahrenheit.

Bundle the herbs, tie with kitchen twine, and place inside the cavity of the chicken. Truss the legs of the chicken with kitchen twine and return the bird breast side up to the roasting pan with a rack. The rack will allow air to circulate under the bird and will help the underside of the chicken to brown.

Rub olive oil all over the outside of the bird and roast for 45 minutes; then baste chicken with the pan juices. Continue roasting for another 10-20 minutes until a meat thermometer inserted into the thickest part of the thigh reads 160 degrees; legs should be loose and juices should be clear.

Let chicken rest for ten minutes before carving; serve with good quality truffle salt.

Pollo Arrosto con Finocchi e Rosmarino
Roast Chicken with Fennel and Rosemary

This is a comforting, easy to make dish. You can pick up the ingredients on the way home from work and have dinner ready in just over an hour. Using bone-in chicken legs or thighs will give your dish more flavor and will help to ensure that the chicken does not dry out.

Wine Pairing
Elvio Cogno Dolcetto d'Alba "Mandorlo," Piemonte

Serves 2-4
· 2 small fennel bulbs with fronds
· Four whole air-dried chicken legs (bone in and skin on) or six bone-in chicken thighs
· 10 sprigs rosemary
· One whole head of garlic cloves in their paper skins
· 4 tablespoons extra-virgin olive oil
· Salt, to taste
· Black pepper, freshly ground to taste

Directions
Preheat oven to 400 degrees Fahrenheit. Line a 13"x18" sheet pan with parchment paper.

Trim off the bottom of the fennel bulbs and then cut the stalks to about two inches from bulbs. You don't need to core the bulbs; they're edible. Next, carefully cut the bulbs lengthwise into 1/2" slices. It's ok to slice through the stalk portion. Reserve a handful of fronds for garnish.

Salt and pepper the chicken on both sides and place each leg on a large sprig of rosemary in the sheet pan. Add two more sprigs of rosemary to the pan. Next, carefully place the sliced fennel between and around the chicken legs, adding a little salt and pepper to taste. Place garlic cloves in their paper skins around the chicken and fennel, and drizzle everything with olive oil.

Place sheet pan on center rack and bake for 25 minutes. If you have a convection fan, you can use that, but keep an eye on the chicken. After 25 minutes, take the garlic cloves out and set aside. Brush chicken and fennel with the olive oil in the pan and return to oven for another 25-30 minutes. The internal chicken temperature will be hotter than needed, but I like my skin crispy. It's also hard to overcook dark meat.

Plate chicken with 2-3 slices of fennel, 2 garlic cloves in their skins, a sprig of fresh rosemary, and fennel fronds.

SECONDI—CARNE

Abbacchio alla Romana
Braised Lamb, Roman Style

This is a spring dish made with suckling lamb, which, unfortunately, is not widely available in the United States. When I can't find a whole lamb shoulder, I use the blade and round bones from the shoulder. I prefer lamb shoulder to leg of lamb; when cooked slow and low, it's juicier. It also shreds nicely the next day into lamb *carnitas*.

Wine Pairing

Alberico Appia Antica Rosso, Lazio

Serves 4

· 4 pounds thick cut lamb blade chops and lamb round bone chops, cut into 3" pieces
· 1 cup dry white wine
· 1 cup white wine vinegar
· 8 garlic cloves, crushed
· 4 sprigs rosemary, stems removed
· 6 anchovies
· *Peperoncino*, to taste
· Salt, to taste
· Black pepper, freshly ground to taste
· 1/4 cup extra-virgin olive oil
· Mint leaves, to garnish

Directions

In a large bowl, marinate lamb in wine, white wine vinegar, garlic, rosemary, anchovies, *peperoncino*, salt, and pepper for 1 hour. Dry lamb pieces with paper towels.

In a Dutch oven heat olive oil over medium-high heat, and sauté lamb pieces in batches until well browned on all sides. Pour off all but a tablespoon of the oil, add marinade, lower heat, cover, and simmer for 50 to 60 minutes. Remove meat to a warm platter. Pour juice and oil through a fine-meshed sieve placed over a gravy separator; discard solids. Return the de-fatted juice to the Dutch oven, add meat and very gently simmer until warm.

Serve on warm plates; garnish generously with mint leaves.

Bistecca alla Fiorentina
Florentine Steak

Going out for a juicy Tuscan steak is something I always do at least once when I'm in Florence. Although it's offered in many restaurants, you really want to go to a restaurant that specializes in grilled meats cooked over a wood grill. Choose a restaurant that's been in Florence since forever. Sostanza, Buca Lapi, Il Latini, and Trattoria Mario are all solid choices. This enormous slab of meat is not something you to want to eat an hour or so before you go to bed, so go for lunch. I usually opt for a late Sunday lunch when the restaurants are less hectic, and the tourists have emptied out.

What is it? *Bistecca alla Fiorentina* is a massive 3" thick, three-pound T-bone steak meant to be shared between two or more people. It comes from a Chianina cow from Valdichiana in Tuscany. Often aged, it's seared to perfection on the outside and served bloody rare. Don't even think about asking for it to be cooked well done. Unfortunately, I don't have a wood grill or access to Valdichiana cows, so I'm going to give you my recipe for a porterhouse cooked *sous-vide* and then seared in a cast iron pan. I like to serve it with a simple rosemary and olive oil marinade and some sautéed spinach on the side.

Wine Pairing
Casanova di Neri Brunello di Montalcino, Toscana

Serves 2-4
· 2 1/2" thick porterhouse steak (this is a t-bone steak cut from the thick end of the sirloin. It has a large juicy strip steak on one side and a smaller tenderloin on the other side).
· 6 sprigs rosemary
· 4 anchovies
· 3 tablespoons Maldon smoked salt
· Black pepper, freshly ground to taste
· Extra-virgin olive oil

Directions
Preheat *sous-vide* water bath to 125 degrees Fahrenheit. (This is approximately the temperature of the water from your kitchen faucet set to its hottest setting).

Season the steak with 1 tablespoon Maldon salt and freshly ground black pepper on both sides. Place in Foodsaver bag with a sprig of rosemary on each side and two anchovies on each side. The anchovies will add a little funk reminiscent of aging. Vacuum seal the bag and place in water bath for 4 hours.

To make the marinade, remove the remaining rosemary leaves from their stems and place into a mortar with 2 tablespoons of Maldon salt and create a little *pesto* or paste. Drizzle with extra virgin olive oil.

About 10 minutes before steak is done, preheat a clean cast iron pan on the stove over high heat.

After four hours, remove steak from water bath and dry very well with paper towels. Brush some olive oil on both sides and sear in the preheated cast iron pan for one minute on each side. Make sure to sear the sides of the steak as well. If you want to be really dramatic, you can also sear the steak with a propane blow torch at the same time. Make sure the stove is off when using a torch.

Place seared meat on a cutting board and cut both sides of the steak into half inch slices, perpendicular to the center bone. Reassemble meat with the bone and serve with rosemary marinade on top.

Bombette di Maiale
Stuffed Pork Rolls

Some of Southern Italy's most picturesque towns are found in the *Valle d'Itria* between Bari and Brindisi in Puglia. Alberobello is famous for its tiny conical domed dwellings called *trulli*; Locorotondo for its whitewashed houses and flowered balconies; and Cisternino for its kasbah-like streets and its *fornelli pronti*, which are butcher shops that will grill your meat for you in their wood-fired stone ovens. The price of your meal is the price of the meat once it's been weighed. You can then take it away as street food or sit down in their restaurant. At the entrance of the butcher shop each *fornello pronto* has a glass case displaying a variety of cuts of meat, sausages, *bombette*, and *gnummarddi*. The latter includes a mixture of lamb's spleen, liver, heart, and lungs that are rolled up and tied with the intestine. They are quite tasty served with sage and lemon. My favorite, however, are the *bombette*, literally 'little bombs' of flavor made with pork neck that is pounded very thin and stuffed with cheese, herbs, and bacon. Each butcher has his favorite stuffing mixtures. My favorite bombette are made with wild boar and stuffed with *pancetta*, arugula, and *caciocavallo*. The following recipe is based on several memorable meals I've eaten in the *fornelli* pronti in Cisternino.

Wine Pairing
Sampietrana Brindisi Riserva, Puglia

Makes 12
· 12 oz pork neck (pork collar)
· 12 thin slices *pancetta* (about 6 oz)
· 6 oz *caciocavallo* cheese, diced into
  small cubes
· Two handfuls of arugula (about 2-3 oz),
  chopped
· Maldon smoked salt, to taste
· Black pepper, freshly ground to taste
· *Peperoncino*, to taste
· 2 garlic cloves, finely chopped

Directions
Preheat oven to 400 degrees Fahrenheit.

Slice pork neck into 1/4" slices, and then pound into 1/8" slices between two sheets of parchment paper. Note that you may have to purchase the whole neck which weighs about 3 pounds. Freeze what you don't use. Luckily this is an inexpensive cut of meat.

Once the meat has been pounded flat, add a pinch of smoked salt (the pancetta can be very salty), and black pepper to taste. Add a little chopped garlic, *peperoncino*, pancetta, cheese, and arugula. Roll up the meat, taking care to tuck in the sides, and secure with a couple of toothpicks. You can also roll up the *bombette* with the *pancetta* on the outside.

Place the bombette on a broiling pan and bake for approximately 30 minutes. Bombette are even better when grilled outside.

Experiment with the meat and fillings. You can substitute veal instead of pork or use chopped parsley and rosemary instead of arugula. The cheeses can also be swapped out; *gorgonzola* is delicious. You can also substitute cured meats, such as *prosciutto* or *capocollo*, in place of pancetta. Some *fornelli pronti* also cover their bombette with bread crumbs and *parmigiano* before grilling.

This is fun food – have fun experimenting.
Buon appetito!

Coda alla Vaccinara
Braised Oxtails (cooked sous-vide for 96 hours)

Coda alla vaccinara is a classic Roman dish that is found on menus all over the city. It translates to oxtail cooked in the manner of the butchers, and it is, at its essence, *cucina povera* or cooking of the poor. Like kidneys and tripe, the oxtail was basically a part of the cow that no one really wanted, so the butchers brought them home and learned how to transform this tough cut into sublime tenderness. When I buy oxtails here at home, I always get a knowing glance and complimentary comment from the butcher; they know what the good stuff is. Oxtails cooked low and slow result in rich, silky meat that literally falls off the bone. Cooking oxtails *sous-vide* for four days ensures that the tough collagen melts out of the meat while, at the same time, guaranteeing that the meat will not be overcooked. Furthermore, this method of cooking allows you to skim off the vast amounts of fat that the oxtails render. In Rome, Nonna Betta in the old Jewish Ghetto and Cul de Sac near the Piazza Navona serve up some pretty tasty *coda alla vaccinara*.

Wine Pairing
Mirafiore Barolo, Piemonte

Serves 4
· 5-6 pounds oxtails, cut into 2" pieces
· 4 tablespoons *doppio concentrato di pomodoro* (double-concentrated tomato paste)
· 1 tablespoon extra-virgin olive oil
· 4 oz *guanciale*, cut into 1/4" lardons
· 1 large yellow onion, finely chopped
· 3 garlic cloves, finely chopped
· *Peperoncino*, to taste
· 1 carrot, finely chopped
· 3 ribs celery, finely chopped
· 1/4 cup parsley, finely chopped
· 1 cup dry red wine

Directions
Day 1
Preheat sous-vide water bath to 140 degrees Fahrenheit.

Bring six quarts of water to boil in a large stock pot. Simmer oxtails in batches for 15 minutes. Skim off any scum that comes to the surface. Drain and dry oxtails well. Reserve 2 cups of the broth. Add 4 tablespoons of tomato paste to reserved broth and refrigerate.

In a Dutch oven heat 1 tablespoon of olive oil and slowly *sauté guanciale* over medium-low heat until its fat has rendered. Remove *guanciale* and set aside.

Increase heat to medium-high and brown oxtails in batches until brown on all sides. This takes time; don't rush the browning process. If the oil starts to smoke, lower heat. Remove oxtails as they brown and place in a large bowl. Let cool for a few minutes and pat dry. Place oxtails into two Foodsaver bags, vacuum seal, and place into water bath for four days (96 hours). There will be a lot of evaporation over the course of four days, so make sure to cover the tub that you are using. I use a 12-quart Rubbermaid commercial plastic food storage container with a lid, into which I cut a hole the size of the diameter of the *sous-vide* cooker. (Check water level several times a day).

Remove and discard all but a tablespoon of the oil in the pot. Lower heat to medium-low and add garlic and *peperoncino* and sauté for 30 seconds; add onions, carrots, parsley and sauté until lightly browned, about 30 minutes. Let vegetables cool; cover and refrigerate.

Day 5

After oxtails have cooked for 96 hours, remove from *sous-vide* bath and remove meat from bones with your hands. Meat should easily fall off the bones. Cover meat and place in refrigerator.

Add bones to the cooked vegetables and add reserved guanciale, red wine, and reserved oxtail broth/tomato paste mixture. Cover and simmer for 3 hours, stirring bones every once in a while. Strain and reserve sauce and vegetables in two different containers in the refrigerator overnight. Save the bones for stock.

Day 6

Skim the hardened fat off the top of the sauce.

Now you have three options:

1) Add sauce to reserved vegetables; add oxtail meat and heat gently.

2) Add sauce to reserved vegetables; heat and blend with an immersion blender before adding oxtail meat.

3) Strain and discard vegetables and heat sauce with the meat.

Garnish with celery leaves and serve on warm plates or in bowls.

*Leftovers are great with rigatoni pasta and *Pecorino Romano*.

Coniglio Brasato alla Ligure
Braised Rabbit Ligurian Style

During Dominican University's summer program in Florence, I enjoy inviting my students and my colleague, Tonia Triggiano, to my apartment for a few family meals. I like introducing the students to traditional Tuscan and Ligurian dishes they have probably never eaten before, such as *cinghiale* (wild boar), *lepre* (hare), and *coniglio* (rabbit). Over the years, I've never had a student shy away from trying these somewhat exotic dishes. On the contrary, they're usually very excited to experiment. Students even squabble over the delicious rabbit heads, with the winners devouring the cheeks and brains. I often serve *coniglio* with *trofie al pesto*. My colleague, Tonia, usually picks up some *cannoli* and *biscotti* from the local *pasticceria* down the street, and wine is poured from the spigots of three-liter boxes. The students are grateful for a free meal and happy to cart away the leftovers, even if it means a slight detour back to their apartments before heading out to the dance clubs for the evening. The following recipe can be divided proportionally.

Wine Pairing
Ka'Mancine Rossese di Dolceaqua "Galeae," Liguria

Serves 12-14
· 3 large rabbits (about 3-pounds each)
· Salt, to taste
· Black pepper, freshly ground to taste
· 6 tablespoons extra-virgin olive oil
· 3 small onions, finely chopped
· 6 garlic cloves, smashed
· 6 bay leaves
· 3 tablespoons thyme, chopped
· 6 sage leaves
· 6 sprigs rosemary + more for garnishing plate
· 3 cups Rossese di Dolceacqua (or other light fruit-driven red wine)
· 12 oz black *gaeta* or *niçoise* olives, un-pitted
· Chicken stock (as needed)
· 6 tablespoons pine nuts, toasted

Directions

If you buy your rabbits with the head on, have the butcher cut the rabbit heads in half, down the center, and cut each rabbit into 10-12 pieces separating the back legs and front legs. Dry well with paper towels; salt and pepper lightly.

In a large Dutch oven, heat olive oil over medium-high heat, and sauté similar-size rabbit pieces in batches until well-browned on all sides (about 10 minutes per batch). Don't rush the browning. Remove rabbit pieces to a plate when browned. Add onions and garlic with a pinch of salt and cook over low heat until softened and translucent. Make sure to scrape up the *fond* at the bottom of the pot with a wooden spoon.

Add bay leaves, thyme, sage, rosemary, and rabbit pieces along with juices and red wine. Cook until red wine reduces by half. Check for salt; cover and cook over low heat for about one hour. Add chicken broth as needed to keep rabbit moist. Add olives during the last 15 minutes of cooking.

Meanwhile, toast pine nuts in a small frying pan until fragrant and slightly browned. Watch closely, as they can burn easily. Remove to a plate.

Transfer rabbit to a warmed serving platter. Garnish with fresh rosemary sprigs and pine nuts. Serve with plenty of broth, and don't forget to remind your guests that the olives are un-pitted.

Coniglio in Agrodolce
Sweet and Sour Rabbit

Agrodolce, which simply means sweet and sour, is a complex mixture of fruits, vegetables, nuts, spices, and vinegar. Sicilian in origin, it is often added to wild game, such as *cinghiale* (wild boar), *Lepre* (wild hare), and *coniglio* (rabbit). It is equally delicious with wild game birds and chicken.

Wine Pairing

Benati, Etna Rosso, Sicilia

Serves 2-4

· 1 large rabbit (3-pounds)
· Salt, to taste
· Black pepper, freshly ground to taste
· 1/2 cup unbleached all-purpose flour
· 1/4 cup + 1 1/2 tablespoon extra-virgin olive oil
· 1 small red onion, finely chopped
· 3 garlic cloves, finely chopped
· 1 carrot, peeled and finely chopped
· 1 small fennel bulb, finely chopped
· 5 ounces *prosciutto*, chopped
· 5 juniper berries
· 5 black peppercorns
· *Peperoncino*, to taste
· 3 sprigs fresh thyme + additional for garnish
· 1 tablespoon cane sugar
· 1/4 cup red wine vinegar
· 2 cups rabbit or chicken stock
· 1/4 cup dried currants
· Slight pinch of ground cinnamon
· 4 tablespoons pine nuts, lightly toasted
· 2 ounces unsweetened dark chocolate
 (85% cacao)
· Fennel fronds
· Zest from 1 orange

Directions

If you buy your rabbits with the head on, have the butcher cut the rabbit heads in half, down the center, and cut each rabbit into 10-12 pieces separating the back legs and front legs. Dry well with paper towels; salt and pepper lightly.

In a large Dutch oven, heat 1/4 cup of olive oil over medium-high heat; dredge rabbit pieces in the flour and sauté in batches until well-browned on both sides (about 5-10 minutes per batch). Remove rabbit pieces to a plate when browned.

Wipe out any burned oil and flour with paper towels. Add 1 1/2 tablespoons of additional oil and sauté vegetables over medium heat until soft, about 5-10 minutes. Add the chopped *prosciutto*, juniper berries, peppercorns, *peperoncino*, thyme and continue to cook for 2 minutes. Return rabbit pieces to the pot; add vinegar, rabbit stock, and sugar. Reduce heat to a low simmer, cover, and cook for 45 minutes.

Meanwhile, toast pine nuts in a small frying pan until fragrant and slightly browned. Remove to a plate. When the rabbit is cooked, add the currants, pinch of cinnamon, 3 tablespoons of the pine nuts, and chocolate, and cook until chocolate melts into the braise.

Transfer rabbit to a warmed serving platter. Garnish with fresh thyme, fennel fronds, orange zest, and 1 tablespoon toasted pine nuts.

Coniglio Ripieno in Porchetta
Rabbit Stuffed in the Manner of Porchetta

Colonnata is an ancient mountain village in the Apuan Alps near the Carrara marble quarries in Tuscany. It's worth a visit; the streets and sidewalks are all made of marble. From the top of the town, you can see the Carrara marble quarries with their endless procession of trucks carting away marble to ship all over the world. From the nearby beaches in Versilia, these mountains look like they're covered in snow. These are the same marble quarries where Michelangelo handpicked the block of marble that would become his *David*.

The town is famous for its *lardo di Colonnata* which is pork fatback seasoned with rosemary, sea salt, and other herbs and spices, and left to cure for months in giant marble tubs. Several producers will invite you into their homes and shops and explain how the *lardo* is cured, and give you a sample or two. It's delicious, and when sliced very thin, literally melts in your mouth. While there are numerous shops that sell *panini con lardo di Colonnata*, my favorite restaurant is the Ristorante Venanzio where *lardo* finds a place with many of the items on the menu, most notably its *coniglio ripieno*, or stuffed rabbit. Unfortunately, authentic *lardo di Colonnata* cannot be imported to the United States. Thankfully a number of local artisans are now curing this delicacy. The following recipe is inspired by my visits to the town of Colonnata and the *coniglio* served at the Ristorante Venanzio.

Wine Pairing

Poliziano Vino Nobile di Montepulciano, Toscana

Serves 4-6

· 1 large rabbit (approximately 3 pounds) deboned, with liver reserved for stuffing
· 1/3 cup fennel fronds, chopped
· 1/3 cup rosemary leaves, finely minced
· 12 sage leaves, chopped
· 3 cloves garlic, thinly sliced
· Grated zest from 1 lemon
· 1 teaspoon kosher salt
· 1/2 teaspoon black pepper, freshly ground
· 1/2 tablespoon fennel seeds
· *Peperoncino*, to taste
· 1/3 cup fennel bulb, chopped
· 2 tablespoons extra-virgin olive oil
· 1/4 pound *lardo di Colonnatta* (or locally produced *lardo*), thinly sliced

Directions

Have your butcher debone a whole rabbit for you. This is not an easy task. Ask him to reserve the liver for the stuffing and the carcass for making stock.

Preheat oven to 375 degrees Fahrenheit.

Place fennel fronds, rosemary, sage, garlic, lemon zest, salt, black pepper, fennel seeds, *peperoncino*, chopped fennel, and olive oil into a food processor and blend into a paste.

Open up the rabbit and cover the inside with the fennel, rosemary, sage paste. Reserve 1 tablespoon for rubbing on the outside of the rabbit.

Rinse the liver in cold water to remove traces of blood and mince. Add liver in a fine line down the center of the rabbit on top of the paste. In Italy, finding a little piece of liver in your slice of porchetta is as important as getting a piece of crispy pork skin.

Carefully roll up the rabbit and place in a 13"x18" sheet pan lined with parchment paper. Rub remaining paste on the outside of the rabbit and cover with slices of *lardo*. Truss rabbit with butchers' twine. If there are any holes in the meat, cut off some extra flaps of meat from the ends and patch before trussing. Bake on the middle shelf of the oven for 35-40 minutes. When the rabbit is done, let it rest for twenty minutes to allow the juices to redistribute throughout the meat.

Remove trussing string, slice and serve with roast potatoes. Slices should be about 1" thick. Pour a little of the juice from the pan over the sliced meat. Serve each slice with a piece of crispy *lardo*.

Coniglio in porchetta is also very good served at room temperature in a *panino* or sandwich. Make sure to brush a little of the pan juices on the inside of the bread and serve with a piece of *lardo*.

Costolette di Abbacchio a Scottadito
Baby Lamb Chops, Scottadito Style

I love lamb chops, and one of my favorite places to eat them is at the Ristorante Piperno in Rome. This venerable restaurant is located in the old Jewish Ghetto and has been around since 1860. It specializes in *la cucina romana*, or Roman, cuisine and specifically Roman Jewish cuisine. My ideal meal there includes *carciofo alla Giudia* (deep fried artichokes), maybe a *filleto fritto di baccalà* (deep fried salt cod), their mouthwatering *costolette di abbacchio a scottadito*, and *insalta di puntarelle* (chicory salad). The last time I was there, I ordered two plates of their *costolette*. At home, I cook my lamb chops sous-vide and then sear them in a blazing hot cast iron pan. In Italian, *scottadito* means burned fingers. This dish is named *scottadito* because the lamb chops are so delicious that it's difficult to resist eating them straight from the grill and burning your fingers.

Wine Pairing

Casale del Giglio Shiraz, Lazio

Serves 2

· 6-8 lamb chops (cut off a rack of lamb)
· 6-8 anchovies
· 6-8 sprigs rosemary
· Maldon smoked salt, to taste
· Black pepper, freshly ground to taste
· Extra-virgin olive oil

Directions

Preheat *sous-vide* water bath to 125 degrees Fahrenheit. (This is approximately the temperature of the water from your kitchen faucet set to its hottest setting).

Season the lamb chops with Maldon smoked salt and freshly ground black pepper on both sides. Divide and place into two Foodsaver bags with 1 sprig of rosemary and one anchovy per lamb chop. Vacuum seal the bag and place in water bath for 2 hours.

About 10 minutes before lamb chops are done, preheat a clean cast iron pan on the stove over high heat.

After two hours, remove chops from water bath and dry very well with paper towels, removing anchovies and rosemary. Brush a little olive oil on both sides of the chops and sear in the preheated cast iron pan for one minute on each side. Feel free to sear the chops with a propane blow torch at the same time. Make sure the stove is off when using a torch.

Serve with *Insalata di Puntarelle alla Romana*.

Cotechino con Lenticchie
Cotechino Sausage with Lentils

Before the Ristorante Paris in Trastevere closed in 2018, I always made it a point to spend New Year's Eve there while I was teaching in Rome during Dominican University's winter interim. Paris always served an elegant multi-course *Cenone di San Silvestro* (New Year's Eve dinner) in their warm and cozy restaurant. When making my reservation, I always asked to be seated in the main dining room near the large marble fireplace. As midnight approached, the waiters would bring out additional glasses of *prosecco* and a portion of *cotechino con lenticchie* for each guest. This seemingly out of place dish, said to bring prosperity in the New Year, hails from Emilia-Romagna. I like it very much, although it's a bit heavy after a ten-course meal. The star of the dish is the sticky *cotechino*, which is made from marbled pork shoulder, pork fat, pork rind, and various "warm" wintery spices, such as cinnamon, nutmeg, allspice, and orange peel. Deliciously satisfying on a chilly winter afternoon.

Wine Pairing

Bisol Valdobbiadene Prosecco Superiore Brut "Jeio," Veneto

Serves 2-4

· 12 ounces *lenticchie dell'Umbria* (Umbrian lentils)
· 12 ounce *cotechino*, precooked
· 2 tablespoons extra-virgin olive oil
· 1 ounce *pancetta*, finely minced
· 2 cloves garlic, crushed
· 1 medium yellow onion, finely chopped
· Salt, to taste
· Black pepper, freshly ground to taste
· 2 sprigs fresh rosemary
· 2 bay leaves
· 2-3 cups vegetable broth

Directions

Soak dried lentils in a bowl of cold water for 2 hours. Drain, rinse in a sieve and set aside.

Place plastic wrapped *cotechino* in a large pot filled with cold water; bring to a boil and simmer 20 minutes until warm. Keep the sausage in the warm water until lentils are cooked.

In a 10" frying pan, heat olive oil, pancetta, and garlic over low heat for 5 minutes until fragrant; remove garlic. Add the chopped onion, salt, pepper, and sauté for 5 minutes until onion is translucent. Increase heat to medium; add the drained lentils, rosemary, a pinch of salt, and bay leaves. Add vegetable broth one ladle at a time until the lentils absorb the broth; simmer over low heat for about 25 minutes until tender.

Remove *cotechino* from the plastic wrap and the natural casing. Do this over a bowl to catch the juice from the sausage; add juice to the lentils. Cut the *cotechino* into 1/2" rounds; dry with paper towels and lightly brown in another skillet over medium heat.

Plate lentils and arrange *cotechino* rounds on top of the lentils.

Porchettina

Pork Shoulder Stuffed with Fennel, Rosemary, Sage and Garlic

Porchetta is a very popular and traditional street food eaten all over Italy. In hill towns all over central Italy, you will see white trucks parked in the main *piazza* on Saturday and Sunday mornings. Those trucks are selling *panini* (sandwiches) filled with slices of savory, mouthwatering pork cut from a whole suckling pig that has been deboned and stuffed with its own liver, along with wild fennel, rosemary, sage, garlic, and lots of salt and pepper. These baby pigs are slow cooked on a spit or roasted over a wood fire for over eight hours. The head is often left on along with all the crispy fat. You can eat these sandwiches even if you aren't hungry; they are so good. My diminutive *porchettina* includes the same herbs and spices found in traditional *porchetta*.

Wine Pairing

Il Borro Pian di Nova, Toscana

Serves 4-6

1 bone-in, skin-on pork shoulder (approximately 8 pounds). I have my butcher cut it in half through the blade bone. I cook one half at a time. It's more than enough for 4-6 people, and I think it looks nicer as a long roast. Freeze half and use this herb blend for a half shoulder.

· 1/3 cup fennel fronds, chopped
· 1/3 cup rosemary leaves, chopped
· 12 sage leaves, chopped
· 6 garlic cloves
· Grated zest from 1 lemon
· 3 teaspoons kosher salt
· 1 tablespoon fennel seeds
· 1 teaspoon *peperoncino*
· 1/2 teaspoon black pepper, freshly ground
· 1/4 cup extra-virgin olive oil

Directions

Using a very sharp knife score the skin into 1/2" diagonal diamond cuts. Be careful not to cut into the meat. I like to do this myself. The butcher will most likely not take as much care to cut evenly. The next step is to butterfly the roast. Use a sharp carving knife; slice through the center of the meat lengthwise so that it opens up like a book. Be careful not to cut all the way to the end, otherwise you'll have two slabs of meat.

Add fennel fronds, rosemary, sage, garlic, lemon zest, salt, fennel seeds, *peperoncino*, black pepper, and olive oil to a food processor and pulse several times. Rub spice and herb mixture all over the pork shoulder inside and out. Make sure you rub the mixture into the diagonal cuts. Truss pork with string to make a nice log shape. Cover with plastic wrap and refrigerate overnight.

Remove pork from refrigerator 2 hours before you plan to roast it. Place meat on a rack in a roasting pan.

Preheat oven to 450 degree Fahrenheit.

Roast pork for 30 minutes. Reduce temperature to 325 degrees and continue cooking for 1-2 hours until the internal temperature of the meat reaches 180 degrees. Transfer roast to serving platter, cover loosely with foil, and let rest 25 minutes before slicing. Serve with roast potatoes and roast fennel.

Stinco di Agnello Brasato
Braised Lamb Shanks

Braised lamb shanks are one of my favorite cold weather Sunday meals. They're hearty, comforting, and delicious. When they are braised low and slow, the collagen and tendons melt into luxurious gelatin. Lamb shanks are, as my anatomy students know, the tibia and fibula of the lamb's lower leg – I often bring these bones into my class and ask my students to identify them. I like to serve *stinco di agnello with puré di cavolfiore* (cauliflower purée) or *risotto allo zafferano* (saffron risotto).

Wine Pairing

Agricola Punica Montessu, Sardegna

Serves 4

· 4 large lamb shanks
· Salt, to taste
· Black pepper, freshly ground to taste
· 1/2 cup extra-virgin olive oil
· 8 cloves garlic, crushed
· 1/2 teaspoon *peperoncino*
· 2 red onions, finely chopped
· 1 tablespoon *doppio concentrat di pomodoro* (double-concentrated tomato paste)
· 2 tablespoons fresh rosemary, chopped
· 1 cup dry white wine
· 1 cup San Marzano tomatoes, crushed
· 1 cup lamb or chicken stock
· Zest from one orange
· 8 sprigs of rosemary to garnish

Directions

Heat oil in a large Dutch oven over medium-high. Salt and pepper lamb shanks and sauté until brown on all sides. Remove lamb and set aside on a plate.

Lower burner to medium-low heat and add the garlic and *peperoncino*; sauté until fragrant. Add onions and sauté until translucent. Add tomato paste, rosemary, wine, tomatoes, and lamb stock and bring to a boil. Add the lamb shanks, cover and simmer over low heat for 3 1/2 hours. Remove lamb shanks from the pot and blend sauce with an immersion blender. Check seasonings.

Serve lamb shanks on warm plates, pour some of the blended sauce over the lamb, garnish with orange zest and fresh rosemary sprigs.

Stracotto di Manzo
Italian Pot Roast

This Italian pot roast is the perfect meal to make on a chilly winter Sunday afternoon. The slow simmering *profumo* (scent) will fill your home with a warm and relaxed ambience. I prefer using fattier chuck roast as opposed to the traditional leaner eye of round, which tends to dry out. It's delicious served over warm *polenta*. But the real reason I like to make it is for the leftovers that, when shredded, make for a delicious pasta sauce with *rigatoni*.

Wine Pairing
Badia al Coltibuono Chianti Classico, Toscana

Serves 6-8
· 1 oz dried *porcini* mushrooms
· 2 cups beef stock
· 4 pounds chuck roast, tied
· Salt to taste
· Black pepper, freshly ground to taste
· 1/4 cup extra-virgin olive oil
· 3 oz *guanciale*, cut into lardons
· 3 garlic cloves, finely minced
· 2 sprigs rosemary leaves, minced
· 1 teaspoon thyme, minced
· 1 bay leaf
· *Peperoncino*, to taste
· 1/2 carrot, peeled and finely chopped
· 1 large yellow onion, finely chopped
· 1 stalk celery, finely chopped
· 1 bottle dry red wine
· 28 oz whole San Marzano tomatoes, crushed
· 3 tablespoon tomato paste
· 1 tablespoon Italian parsley, finely chopped

Directions
Soak the *porcini* mushrooms in 1 cup of warm beef stock until softened, about 30 minutes. Strain liquid through a sieve and reserve. Dry the pot roast well and season with salt and freshly ground black pepper.

Heat oil in a large Dutch oven over medium-high heat. Brown roast on all sides until well browned, about 15-20 minutes. Remove roast to a plate and set aside. Pour out browning fat but leave the *fond* on the bottom of the pan.

Add *guanciale* and cook over low heat until it renders its fat and becomes crispy. Add garlic, rosemary, thyme, bay leaf, *peperoncino*, carrot, onion, and celery to the pot and cook over medium-low heat until onions are translucent, about 10 minutes.

Add wine, increase heat, and reduce by half, about 15 minutes. Return roast to pot with juices, crushed tomatoes, tomato paste, *porcini* mushrooms, beef stock, and the stock used to soak the mushrooms. Bring to a low simmer and cook covered for 2-3 hours until meat is tender. Turn meat in sauce every 20 minutes.

When meat is cooked, transfer to a plate and cover with foil for 15 minutes. Skim off as much fat as possible from surface of the sauce, check seasonings, and continue to cook over medium heat for a few minutes to thicken sauce.

Serve over warm *polenta*, mashed potatoes, or *puré di cavolfiore*. Garnish with freshly chopped parsley.

Vitello Tonnato
Veal with Tuna Sauce

This is a delicious appetizer from Piedmont that can easily become a main course with a larger serving. Traditionally made with veal eye of round, it's easy to prepare and makes for an elegant summer lunch. I make it with pork tenderloin, which is less expensive than veal and perhaps more humane. Whether you use veal or pork, you can cook either meat *sous-vide* and then sear it in a cast iron pan. Perfect beach food from a region of Italy with no access to the sea.

Wine Pairing
Villa Sparina Gavi del Comune di Gavi, Piemonte

Serves 4-8
· 1 pound pork tenderloin, cut in half crosswise
· Salt, to taste
· Black pepper, freshly ground to taste
· 1 tablespoon olive oil
· 6 ounces good quality jarred tuna in olive oil, drained
· 4 anchovies
· 4 tablespoons capers, drained and rinsed
· 1 shallot, chopped
· 2 tablespoons fresh lemon juice
· 4 hardboiled egg yolks
· 3/4 cup extra virgin olive oil
· Garnish with celery leaves, Italian parsley, large caperberries, and thinly sliced radishes

Directions
Preheat *sous-vide* water bath to 125 degrees Fahrenheit. Place pork tenderloin into a FoodSaver bag, vacuum seal, and place into water bath for 1 hour.

About 10 minutes before the pork is done, preheat a clean cast iron pan on the stove over medium-high heat. Remove pork from the *sous-vide* bath and dry well with paper towels. Add 1 tablespoon of olive oil to the pan and sear the pork on all sides for 4-5 minutes. Place pork in the refrigerator for an hour.

Meanwhile, place tuna, anchovies, capers, shallot, lemon juice, salt, and egg yolks in a food processor. Pulse until chopped; slowly pour in olive oil in a thin stream until emulsified.

Slice pork thinly against the grain. Arrange pork on a platter and cover with tuna sauce. Garnish with celery leaves, parsley, large caperberries, and thinly sliced radishes.

CONTORNI

Fagioli al Fiasco
Beans in a Flask

The first time I ate white bean *bruschetta* (toasted Tuscan bread) rubbed with garlic and covered with *cannellini* beans drizzled with fresh extra-virgin olive oil, was at the Ristorante Il Cantinone near the Piazza Santo Spirito in Florence. It was a simple, memorable meal of assorted meats and vegetables on toasted bread. Years later, in a shop on the Piazza dell' Anfiteatro in Lucca, I found a glass flask specifically made for cooking beans. I always seem to return home with my bags packed with kitchen gear.

Wine Pairing

La Braccesca Rosso di Montepulciano "Sabazio," Toscana

Serves 2-4

· 1/2 pound dried *cannellini* beans
· 3 tablespoons extra-virgin olive oil
· 2 cloves garlic
· 4-5 sage leaves
· 1 teaspoon salt
· 1/2 teaspoon white pepper, freshly ground

Directions

Soak beans overnight. The next day drain and rinse beans and place in a glass flask or *fiasco* with oil, sage, garlic, and white pepper. Cover with 2-3 inches water and insert a rolled-up cloth napkin in the opening of the flask to allow steam to be released.

Place the flask over a heat diffuser and simmer over low heat for 1-2 hours. Beans should be tender but firm. Drain when done; drizzle with good quality olive oil.

Can be served as a side dish with meat and poultry, over toasted country bread rubbed with garlic as an *antipasto*, or in a salad with oil-packed tuna and red onions.

Caponata Siciliana
Eggplant and Fennel Caponata

This delicious *contorno* evokes Sicily's Arab past. The Arabs brought the tradition of *agrodolce* (sweet and sour) to the island in the ninth century. The secret is to add the cinnamon, cocoa, sugar, and vinegar sparingly so that these ingredients contribute to a greater whole without calling too much attention to themselves. *Caponata* is an excellent accompaniment to broiled lamb and pork chops. It can also be served as an *antipasto* over toasted bread.

Wine Pairing

Rio Favara Moscato di Noto Mizzica, Sicilia

Serves 4-6

· 3 tablespoons dried currants
· 4 tablespoons pine nuts
· 6 tablespoons extra-virgin olive oil
· 1 large red onion, chopped
· 3 garlic cloves, sliced
· 2 small fennel bulbs, chopped
· *Peperoncino*, to taste
· 2 medium eggplants, chopped
· 2 teaspoons cane sugar
· 1/2 teaspoon ground cinnamon
· 1/2 teaspoon cocoa powder
· 2 teaspoons fresh thyme
· 14 oz can of whole San Marzano tomatoes; cut tomatoes into strips (save juice for another use)
· 1/4 cup red balsamic vinegar
· Salt, to taste
· Black pepper, freshly ground to taste
· Zest from a navel orange

Directions

Cover currants with the balsamic vinegar and set aside to soften. After 15 minutes, drain; reserve vinegar.

In a small frying pan, toast the pine nuts; remove to a small plate. Chop onion, fennel, and eggplant into 1/2" cubes.

In a 12" frying pan, heat the olive oil over medium heat and sauté the onion, garlic, fennel, eggplant, and *peperoncino*. Add salt and pepper to taste and cook until vegetables have softened, about 10 minutes. Add sugar, 3 tablespoons of the pine nuts, currants, cocoa powder, thyme, cinnamon, tomatoes, and vinegar, and bring to a boil; lower heat and simmer for 5-10 minutes; remove from heat and allow to cool to room temperature.

Garnish with 1 tablespoon toasted pine nuts and orange zest.

Fave con Lardo di Colonnata
Fava Beans with Cured Pork Fatback

One of the first things that I do the morning after I arrive in Florence is go to the Mercato Sant'Ambrogio in the Piazza Ghiberti to stock up on some basic items to have on hand in the *frigo* (refrigerator). I love this market; it's smaller than the Mercato Centrale and caters to locals rather than to tourists. My first stop is always La Botteghina dell'Augusto di Formigli Ilaria. This friendly *alimentari* has a wonderful selection of *salumi*, homemade pasta sauces, local cheeses, olives, and fresh bread. Next stop, the vegetables vendors outside the pavilion, where I let them pick out their best tomatoes, *porcini* mushrooms, and fresh *fava* beans. I love the mild, creamy flavor of fresh *fava* beans. It takes a bit of time and effort to prepare them but it's so worth it. I like to serve them with *lardo di Colonnata* and a little grated *Pecorino Toscano*.

Wine Pairing

Montenidoli Vernaccia di San Gimignano Tradizionale, Toscana

Serves 2-4

· 4 pounds unshelled *fava* beans
· 2 tablespoon extra-virgin olive oil
· 2 small shallots, finely chopped (approximately 2 tablespoons)
· 2 oz *lardo di Colonnata*
· Salt, to taste
· Black pepper, freshly ground
· *Pecorino Toscano*, freshly grated

Directions

To shell the *fava* bean pods, twist pods and run your finger up the seam; the beans will fall out easily. Four pounds will yield approximately 2 cups.

Blanch beans for one minute in boiling water, then place in ice bath. Drain beans and remove skins by making a little opening on one end with your fingernail; squeeze the beans out.

Heat olive oil over low heat and add shallots. Cook until soft, about 5 minutes. Do not brown. Add fava beans and warm for an additional 5 minutes over low heat. Turn off burner, add *lardo*, and serve on warm plates. Top with freshly grated *Pecorino Toscano*. Fava beans are also delicious with shaved truffles.

Funghi Trifolati
Sautéed Mushrooms

Sautéed mushrooms always remind me of Umbria, and Orvieto in particular, where I've eaten them many times with grilled meat and roasted fowl. They add a wonderful earthy note to any meal in all seasons. Although *porcini* mushrooms are traditional, a mix of wild mushrooms such as chanterelles and morels work just as well.

Wine Pairing

Antonelli Trebbianno Spoletino "Trebium," Umbria

Serves 4-6

· 1 pound *porcini* mushrooms, roughly chopped
· 1 tablespoon extra-virgin olive oil
· 1 tablespoon butter
· Salt, to taste
· Black pepper, freshly ground to taste
· 2 shallots, finely minced
· 1 garlic clove, smashed
· 1 tablespoon parsley, finely chopped
· 5-6 fresh sage leaves

Directions

In a 12" sauté pan, heat olive oil and butter over medium-high heat. Add mushrooms, salt and pepper. When the mushrooms release their juice, add shallots, garlic, parsley, and sage leaves. Remove from heat when the shallots are translucent and soft; discard garlic. Serve immediately.

Patate al Forno con Aglio e Rosmarino
Roast Potatoes with Garlic and Rosemary

Roast potatoes are an excellent accompaniment to grilled and roasted meats and fowl. I prefer them to mashed potatoes, and they are so much easier to make. Some recipes call for blanching the potatoes first to get a crunchier crust. I skip that step and still get tasty results.

Serves 4-6
· 1 1/2 pounds yellow fingerling potatoes
· 1 tablespoon rosemary, finely minced
· 1 head of garlic cloves in their paper skins
· 3 tablespoons of extra-virgin olive oil
· Salt, to taste
· Black pepper, freshly ground to taste

Directions
Preheat oven to 400 degrees.

Cut the potatoes in half lengthwise and then crosswise into 1" long pieces. Place in a 13" x 18" sheet pan lined with parchment paper. Add chopped rosemary, garlic cloves, and olive oil. Generously salt and pepper; toss well to mix. Turn potato pieces face down and bake for 30 minutes on a middle shelf. After baking for 30 minutes, remove garlic and reserve. Continue baking potatoes until nicely browned and crispy. Serve with reserved garlic.

Polenta
Italian Cornmeal

Although I occasionally like warm creamy *polenta*, I generally prefer it grilled. Once it's cooked, I pour it into three or four small greased molds. When cooled, I simply flip out the molded *polenta* and slice it with a very sharp knife. I then grill it in a ridged cast iron frying pan, making a half turn on both sides midway through grilling to get some nice cross marks. The Mill at Janie's Farm, 80 miles south of Chicago sells a variety of organic and locally grown white and yellow corn flours used to make *polenta*. Grilled white *polenta* slices are great with *baccalà mantecato* and are quite popular in Venice. An excellent wine bar that serves *polenta* like this is El Sbarlefo in Cannaregio.

Serves 4-6
- 2 cups medium course *polenta* (white or yellow)
- 7 cups cold water
- 1 tablespoon kosher salt
- Additional boiling water if needed

Directions
Bring water to a rapid boil in a large pot, add salt. Slowly add *polenta* while stirring with a wooden spoon. Reduce heat to medium-low. Always stir in the same direction to prevent lumps. Stir continuously for approximately 30 minutes until polenta is soft and creamy and begins to pull away from the sides of the pan. Add additional boiling water if the *polenta* is thick but not pulling away from sides.

Pour onto warm plates and top with *baccalà alla vicentina* (codfish Vicenza-style), *coda alla vaccinara* (braised oxtails), *stracotto di manzo* (Italian pot roast), or *stinco di agnello* (braised lamb shanks.

Puntarelle alla Romana
Chicory Roman Style

In Rome, *puntarelle* is a very popular *contorno* or side dish in the winter when they are in season. These bitter greens belong to the chicory family and are difficult to find in the United States. They are prepared by stripping off the leaves and cutting the stalks into thin strips, that are then placed in ice water until they curl up. In the Campo de' Fiori market there is a hawker/comedian that sells inexpensive wire gadgets that strips the leaves and cuts the stalks in one swift motion. He's an entertaining presence in the center of the square. If you watch his act for a few minutes, I guarantee that you will buy something from him. At home, I use similar tasting Belgian endives that I cut into thin strips.

Wine Pairing

Castello della Sala Orvieto Classico Superiore "San Giovanni della Sala," Umbria

Serves 2-4

· 2 Belgian endives, cut lengthwise into thin strips
· 2 tablespoons extra-virgin olive oil
· 4 anchovies
· 1 garlic clove, smashed
· 2 teaspoons white wine vinegar
· Salt, to taste
· Black pepper, freshly ground to taste

Directions

Soak Belgian endive strips in ice water for 30-60 minutes until crisp; they will not curl like *puntarelle*. Dry well.

In a small bowl, combine olive oil, anchovies, garlic, vinegar, salt, and pepper. Mash the anchovies with a wooden spoon. Add strips of Belgian endive, mix well and serve.

Puré di Cavolfiore
Cauliflower Purée

Puréed cauliflower is a light and healthy alternative to mashed potatoes. It goes well with all sorts of grilled and braised meats, such as *costolette di abbacchio allo scottadito* (lamb chops), *stracotto di manzo* (pot roast), and *stinco di agnello* (lamb shanks). It's also super easy to make.

Serves 2-4
· 1 large head cauliflower
· 3 tablespoons unsalted butter
· 1 teaspoon kosher salt
· 1/4 teaspoon white pepper, freshly ground

Directions

Add 2 cups of water to a pot with a steamer insert and bring to a boil.

Remove leaves from the cauliflower, and cut 1/4" off the bottom. There really is no need to core the cauliflower. Break up the florets into small pieces and place in the steamer insert. Cover and steam for about 10-12 minutes. Don't over steam; it should have a little texture and bite.

Remove cauliflower and place in a food processor. Add ½ cup of steaming liquid to the processor and blend. Stop to scrape down sides and check texture. It should have the loose consistency of a purée. It should not be watery. Add butter, salt, and white pepper. Check seasonings and serve immediately.

Sauté di Spinaci
Sautéed Spinach

In Italy I often see small balls of blanched spinach for sale in the supermarkets and specialty shops. It's a very convenient way to buy your spinach. It keeps in the refrigerator for several days until you're ready to cook it. Then, you simply sauté and serve it with no watery mess. Spinach is an excellent accompaniment to grilled meats and fish as well as braised dishes.

Serves 4

· 2 pounds baby spinach leaves, washed
· 4 tablespoons extra-virgin olive oil
· 4 garlic cloves, crushed
· *Peperoncino*, to taste
· 4 anchovies

Directions

Bring 8 quarts of water to a rapid boil; add 2 tablespoons of salt. In a large bowl, add several handfuls of ice and cold water. Place near the stove.

Place 1 pound of spinach leaves in the boiling water for one minute. Strain spinach with a kitchen spider and place in the ice bath to stop the cooking process and to keep the leaves bright green. Pour into a colander under cold running water and repeat with second batch of spinach.

Once the ice has melted, squeeze the spinach into four balls, squeezing out as much water as you can. This takes time. Squeeze the spinach between your palms and your fingers over and over again until you have 4 small balls approximately 2 1/2" in diameter. Each ball will weigh approximately 3 1/2 oz.

When you are ready to cook the spinach, chop it roughly. Warm olive oil over low heat in a 10" frying pan with garlic, *peperoncino*, and anchovies and cook slowly until garlic is fragrant and anchovies have begun to dissolve. You can help them along by mashing them with a wooden spoon. Add spinach and sauté over medium heat until warm. Toss and separate spinach until well coated; remove garlic and serve.

You can, of course, sauté the spinach balls one at a time; simply divide the ingredients accordingly.

FORMAGGI

Tagliere di Formaggi Erborinati
Blue Cheese Board

Cheese tasting can be a lot of fun, especially if you are with a group of creative people. My go-to person at the cheese counter at Eataly, Chicago, is Amber Consolino who is very knowledgeable about the cheeses she sells. I recently asked her to help me curate a plate of Italian blue cheeses to serve as the final course at one of my Sunday lunches. The cheeses she chose ran from mild marbled cow's milk cheese, to a crunchy caramelly water buffalo cheese, to a smoky, throat burning goat's milk cheese. At the Sunday lunch where I served these cheeses, my guests included Frank Spidale, who teaches painting with me at Dominican University, his wife and pastry chef Nancy Carey, Dave Pabellon, who teaches graphic design at Dominican, and his wife and artist Meaghan Pabellon. We tasted the cheeses in the order recommended by Amber. I first asked everyone to describe the cheeses and then to pair them with musicians. While I was thinking blues and jazz, my friends had other thoughts, and the music genre somehow shifted to r&b and hip hop.

Wine Pairing
Montecariano Valpolicella Ripasso,
Veneto

Erborinato San Carlo
Piemonte (cow's milk) – Alicia Keys
soft, toasted, efflorescent, minerally, round, smooth,
coffee, floral

Blu del Monceniso
Piemonte (cow's milk) – Lizzo
creamy, rich mouthfeel, decadent, buttery, velvety, chewy

Blue di Bufala
Lombardia (water buffalo's milk) – Khalid
grainy, crystalized, explosive, light, airy, crunchy,
caramelly, balanced acidity

Gorgonzola
Lombardia (cow's milk) – Cardi B
oregano, citric, grassy, soft, astringent, tangy, dry end
notes, peppery

Erborinati di Capra
Piemonte (goat's milk) – Gil Scott-Heron
mouth puckering, tobacco, smoky, throat burning,
medicinal, tastes like a hospital, 150 proof

In Italian, the words *blu* and *erborinato* are both used for blue cheese. *Erborinato* comes from the word *erborin*, which is parsley in the Milanese dialect. The idea is, that the blue-green veins resulting from the introduction of *penicillium* into the cheese look like parsley.

Tagliere di Pecorini Misti
Mixed Sheep's Milk Cheese Board

I've always found that desserts signal the finality of a meal, while a cheese course encourages continued conviviality and wine consumption. For this Sunday lunch, I asked Amber Consolino, at Eataly, Chicago, to curate a plate of assorted *pecorino* cheeses. She generously helped me pick out a variety of sheep milk cheeses from five different regions in Italy. After dinner, I asked my guests to describe the flavor notes that they tasted for each cheese on the cheese board. The adjectives were thoughtfully considered and included front-end and back-end tastes, such as "grassy," "acidic," "caramelly," "pop rock salt," "nutty," "cake vs cookies," "marshmallow," "gelatinous," and "egg yolky". In the end, however, we decided to attribute an Italian artist's name to the cheeses. These were the results.

Wine Pairing
Le Terrazze Rosso Conero,
Le Marche

Pecorino DOP Valsana
Sicilia (sheep's cheese) – Giotto

Pecorini Guffanti
Basilicata (sheep's cheese) – Masaccio

Caseificio Il Fiorino
Toscana (sheep's cheese) – Tiepolo

Nuvola di Pecora Kinara
Campania (sheep's cheese) – Masolino

Pecorino Canestrato al Tartuffo
Lombardia (sheep's cheese) – Caravaggio

After our tasting was done, I brought out an assortment of Italian honeys, spicy fruit *mostarde* (mustard with preserved fruits), and grappa. What a great way to end a great meal on a Sunday afternoon.

Tagliere di Formaggi Misti
Mixed Cheese Board

For an avid cook that can determine the main ingredients, spices, and herbs in most dishes, I have to confess I'm at a loss for evocative adjectives when trying to describe the distinctive flavors of cheese; that's why I have my friends do it for me. For this *pranzo della domenica* (Sunday lunch), Amber Consolino, at Eataly, Chicago, curated the following a mixed cheese board for me. After tasting a variety cheeses, I decided on a selection made from cow, goat, sheep, and buffalo milk, all produced in Northern Italy. My guests and I tasted these cheeses by themselves and, then, with a slice of bread. We all decided that this selection of cheese was too flavorful and assertive to pair with honey or *mostarde*. The following are the tasting notes that we came up with.

Wine Pairing
La Kiuva Arnad Montjovet, Valle d'Aosta

Camembert
Alta Langa, Piemonte (cow, sheep and goat's milk) lemony, bright, tangy, summer, rustic, earthy, fresh, warm and fuzzy, smells like the farm

Quadrello di Bufala
4 Portoni, Lombardia (water buffalo milk) smoky, grassy, mushrooms, smooth, creamy, sweet

Cusiè in Foglie di Castagno
Beppino Occelli, Piemonte (goat's milk) *dulce di leche*, caramelly, honey, sweet, creamy, clover blossoms, nutty

Sottocenese all Tartufo
Veneto (cow's milk, truffles) garlicky, ashy, mild, smooth, cinnamony, nutmeg

Erborinato, San Carlo Guffanti
Piemonte (cow's milk) luxurious, complex, rich, dark, coffee, spicy, barn, starts with a kick and ends with a smooth finish

LE PIZZE

L'Impasto per la Pizza
Pizza Dough

The following recipe, adapted from Peter Reinhardt's *American Pie*, makes a good *Napoletana* (Naples style) pizza dough. I generally use Marino "00" Bio flour or Antimo Caputo "00" flour. Alternately, you can also use King Arthur's unbleached all-purpose flour. I'm a big fan of SAF Red dry instant yeast which, when stored in the freezer, keeps for several years.

It is more precise to weigh out the ingredients as opposed to using measuring cups and spoons. I prefer to use the metric system when baking and weigh out all the ingredients in the bowl of my Kitchen Aid stand mixer. You will need a kitchen scale that converts to grams. Set the bowl on the scale, reset the scale to zero, and slowly add the ingredients by weight.

Makes four 170 gram (6 oz) dough balls
· 425 grams "00" flour
· 4 grams SAF Red instant yeast
· 14 grams kosher salt
· 250 grams (250 ml) cool water

Directions

Mix the dry ingredients in the bowl of a stand mixer with a silicone spatula, add water. Attach a dough hook to your stand mixer and mix at a low speed for 4-5 minutes until the ingredients are combined into a rough ball. Let the dough rest for 5 minutes and then continue mixing at a medium-low speed for another 2 minutes. If the dough is too sticky, add more flour by the tablespoon. If the dough is too dry, add water by the tablespoon.

Transfer dough to a floured surface and shape into a ball. Place dough in a bowl brushed with olive oil; roll dough ball to coat all sides. Cover bowl and let dough rest at room temperature for 30 minutes. After 30 minutes, place bowl in the refrigerator overnight. Dough will be good for up to 3 days. Cold overnight fermentation improves the dough's flavor and texture.

The next day, take the dough out of the refrigerator two hours before you plan to bake your pizzas. Carefully transfer dough onto a floured surface and divide into four equal pieces. Take care not to degas the dough. Shape each piece into a ball and place on a parchment-paper-lined sheet pan. Brush with a little olive oil and cover with plastic wrap until ready to bake.

One of the secrets to great pizza is a super-hot oven. Wood burning ovens can reach 800 degrees Fahrenheit and can cook a pizza in 1-2 minutes. In my home I have a large professional FibraMent Baking Stone placed on the bottom shelf of my oven. I preheat the oven to 550 degrees Fahrenheit for two hours before baking pizzas.

When you are ready to bake, build your pizza on a wooden pizza peel dusted with rice flour. (Rice flour has a very high burning point and won't smoke when it hits the stone.)

Carefully stretch and shape the dough ball with your hands into a 9" round disk. Place the dough on the back of your hands and let gravity and the weight of the dough assist in stretching it. The *cornicione*, or outside edge, should be a little thicker than the center of the pizza. Place your ingredients on top of the pizza and slide onto the pizza stone. Pizzas are done when the cornicione and bottom are golden brown. Don't be afraid of a little charring; those black spots taste good.

Remove pizza from the oven with a metal pizza peel (metal peels are thinner and easier to slide under the pizza). Transfer baked pizza back onto the wooden peel. Allow pizza to relax for 2-3 minutes before serving.

Pizza al Nero di Seppia
Pizza with Cuttlefish Ink

Several years ago, I thought I was very clever when I made black cuttlefish pizzas on Halloween. Then, I spent a summer in Bari and realized squid and cuttlefish pizzas are very popular in Puglia. For black pizza dough, mix 2 ounces of black cuttlefish ink with 2 ounces of hot water; then add the cool water and follow the recipe for the *Napoletana* pizza dough. Keep in mind that one pound of octopus cooked sous-vide will yield about 7 ounces after cooking.

I like adding spicy olive oil on top of this pizza. To make it, simply add a handful of *peperoncino* to a cup of extra-virgin olive oil, cover and let sit for a few days.

Wine Pairing
Felline Vermentino, Puglia

Serves 2
· 2 "black" pizza dough balls, 170 gram (6 oz) each
· 3 oz smoked *scarmorza*, cut into 1/4" cubes
· 14 oz can of San Marzano tomatoes, drained and cut into strips
· 8 oz octopus (pre-cooked sous-vide), thinly sliced (See page 114 for sous-vide instructions)
· 4 Fresno peppers, cut crosswise (seeds removed)
· Maldon smoked salt, to taste
· Spanish *pimentón* (optional)
· Spicy extra-virgin olive oil

Directions
Build your pizza on a wooden pizza peel dusted with rice flour.

Top pizza with the smoked *scarmorza*, tomatoes, octopus, and Fresno peppers. Slide pizza onto the pizza stone with the wooden pizza peel. Bake until dough is bubbly and a little charred on the edges. Note that it can be difficult to see the char on a black pizza.

Remove pizza from the oven with a metal pizza peel and transfer baked pizza back onto the wooden peel. Add Maldon smoked salt, a sprinkling of *pimentón*, and a drizzle of *peperoncino* infused extra-virgin olive oil.

Let the pizza relax for 2-3 minutes before serving

Pizza al Salmone Affumicato
Pizza with Smoked Salmon

I'm a big fan of salad pizzas. One of my favorites is pizza bianca (white pizza with no tomatoes) made with *rucola* (arugula), *prosciutto*, and *Parmigiano*. Simply cook the pizza dough with a little olive oil and add the rucola, prosciutto and *Parmigiano* after the pizza has baked. *Pizza bianco al salmone affumicato* is a variation on this pizza using smoked salmon.

Wine Pairing

Abbazia di Novacella Kerner,
Trentino Alto-Adige

Serves 2

· 2 pizza dough balls, 170 grams (6 oz) each
· Extra-virgin olive oil
· Maldon smoked salt
· 2 balls fresh *burrata* cheese
· 2 oz red onions, very thinly sliced
· 2 oz fennel, thinly sliced
· Fresh *rucola*
· 4-6 oz smoked salmon
· Fennel pollen

Directions

Build your pizza on a wooden pizza peel dusted with rice flour.

Brush olive oil on top of the pizza and add a sprinkling of smoked salt. Slide pizza onto the pizza stone with the wooden pizza peel. Bake until dough is bubbly and a little charred on the edges.

Remove pizza from the oven with a metal pizza peel and transfer the baked pizza back onto the wooden peel. Top pizza with the *burrata*, onions, fennel, *rucola*, and smoked salmon. Add a sprinkling of fennel pollen, and a drizzle of extra-virgin olive oil.

Allow pizza to relax for 2-3 minutes before serving.

Pizza con Bottarga, Carciofini Grigliati, e Gamberi

Pizza with Bottarga, Grilled Artichokes and Shrimp

I first had pizza with bottarga in the picturesque city of Alghero on the northwest coast of Sardinia. For this recipe you will need whole Bottarga (salt cured fish roe from a grey mullet). Bottarga can be found online or at Eataly. I also recommend buying a jar of small grilled artichokes in olive oil made by DeCarlo.

Wine Pairing

Jankara Vermentino di Gallura, Sardegna

Serves 2

· 2 pizza dough balls, 170 grams (6 oz) each
· 6 oz fresh mozzarella, sliced
· 6 small artichoke hearts, sliced
· 12 small shrimp, shelled, deveined
  and sliced in half lengthwise
· 2 oz bottarga, shaved

Directions

Build your pizza on a wooden pizza peel dusted with rice flour.

Top pizza with sliced *mozzarella*, sliced artichoke hearts, and shrimp. Slide pizza onto the pizza stone with the wooden pizza peel. Bake until dough is golden brown, bubbly, and a little charred on the edges.

Remove pizza from the oven with a metal pizza peel and transfer cooked pizza back onto the wooden peel and shave *bottarga* directly on the warm pizza (I use a truffle shaver).

Allow pizza to relax for 2-3 minutes before serving.

Pizza con Scamorza Affumicata, Speck e Rucola

Pizza with Smoked Scamorza, Smoked Prosciutto and Arugula

This is a salad pizza that is a cousin to pizza al *salmone affumicato*. *Speck* hails from the South Tyrol region of Northern Italy; it is a boned ham, cured with aromatic herbs and spices, smoked, and then air-dried. You certainly could make this pizza with *prosciutto*, but *speck* adds a smoky assertiveness. *Scamorza affumicata* is a dry, firm, smoked cheese from southern Italy that's similar to low-moisture *mozzarella*. This pizza is a marriage between Northern and Southern Italy; everyone likes smoke.

Wine Pairing
Alois Lageder Lagrein Riserva Conus, Alto-Adige

Serves 2
· 2 pizza dough balls, 170 grams (6 oz) each
· 1 cup grated *scamorza affumicata*
· 2 fresh tomatoes, cut into 1/4" slices
· 1/4 cup freshly grated *Parmigiano-Reggiano*
· 8 slices thinly sliced *speck*
· Fresh *rucola*

Directions
Build your pizza on a wooden pizza peel dusted with rice flour.

Add 1/2 cup grated *scamorza affumicata*, top with 4-5 tomato slices, half of the Parmigiano-Reggiano, and two slices of *speck*. Slide pizza onto the pizza stone with the wooden pizza peel. Bake until dough is bubbly and a little charred on the edges.

Remove pizza from the oven with a metal pizza peel and transfer the baked pizza back onto the wooden peel. Top pizza with a handful of *rucola* and two more slices of *speck*. Add a drizzle of extra-virgin olive oil.

Allow pizza to relax for 2-3 minutes before serving.

BRODI

Brodo di Carne
Beef Stock

As with chicken and fish, save the bones! Place them in plastic freezer bags until you have enough to make your stock. I make stock from everything, and this recipe works just as well for pork, veal, and lamb.

Makes 2 quarts

· 4 pounds meaty beef bones, or combination of beef and veal bones, fat removed.
· 1 large yellow onion, quartered
· 2 stalks of celery, cut into 2" pieces
· 1 large carrot, cut into 2" pieces
· 2 bay leaves
· 8 sprigs Italian parsley
· 1 teaspoon whole black peppercorns
· 4 quarts cold water
· Salt to taste (at the end of cooking)

Directions

Place beef bones, onion, celery, carrot, bay leaves, parsley, and peppercorns in a large stock pot and cover with cold water. Bring almost to a boil over high heat and immediately reduce to a low simmer for four hours uncovered until liquid has reduced by half. Periodically skim off any scum that rises to the top. Be careful not to stir the pot, as that will create a cloudy stock.

For a darker, richer stock, in a pre-heated 400-degree Fahrenheit oven roast beef bones and vegetables separately until browned. Use two different sheet pans covered with parchment. Add 1 tablespoon of olive oil to the beef bones and 1 tablespoon of oil to the vegetables. Toss with a little salt. Keep a close eye on the vegetables; you want them to brown but not char; otherwise your stock will taste bitter.

Strain stock through a fine-mesh strainer into a clean saucepan. Let cool and refrigerate overnight. The next day skim any congealed fat off the surface and place into airtight plastic pint containers. The stock should be very gelatinous. Freeze until needed. Stock can be stored in the freezer for up to four months.

Brodo di Pollo
Chicken Stock

This recipe works equally well with all kinds of fowl, such as duck, goose, and turkey; just make sure the proportions are approximately the same. Save bones and broken-down carcasses in freezer bags until you have enough to make your stock.

Makes 2 quarts

· 4-5 pounds chicken carcasses,
  or mix of chicken backs, wings, and legs
· 1 large yellow onion, quartered
· 2 stalks of celery, cut into 2" pieces
· 1 large carrot, cut into 2" pieces
· 2 bay leaves
· 8 sprigs Italian parsley
· 3-4 sprigs of thyme
· 1 teaspoon whole black peppercorns
· 4 quarts cold water
· Salt, to taste (at the end of cooking)

Directions

Place chicken bones, onion, celery, carrot, bay leaves, parsley, thyme, and peppercorns in a large stock pot and cover with cold water. Bring almost to a boil over high heat and immediately reduce to a low simmer for four hours uncovered until liquid has reduced by half. Periodically skim off any scum that rises to the top. Be careful not to stir the pot, as that will create a cloudy stock.

For a darker richer stock, in a pre-heated 400-degree Fahrenheit oven roast chicken and vegetables separately until browned. Use two different sheet pans covered with parchment. Add 1 tablespoon of olive oil to the chicken and 1 tablespoon of olive oil to the vegetables. Toss with a little salt. Keep a close eye on the vegetables; you want them to brown but not char; otherwise your stock will taste bitter.

Strain stock through a fine-mesh strainer into a clean saucepan. Let cool and refrigerate overnight. The next day skim any congealed fat off the surface and place into airtight plastic pint containers. The stock should be very gelatinous. Freeze until needed. Stock can be stored in the freezer for up to four months.

Brodo di Pesce
Fish Stock

Get into the habit of saving your fish carcasses, shrimp shells, lobster shells, etc. in plastic freezer bags until you have enough to make your stock. Or, you can add them to a couple pounds of fish heads and bones available from your fishmonger. As with most stocks, more types of bones and shells will add more complexity to your stock. Use the bones from mild white fish only, such as sea bass, red snapper, sea bream, and cod. Do not use flat fish, such as flounder or sole; or oily fish, such as salmon, tuna, bluefish, sardines, or mackerel, as these will make your stock bitter and overly fishy.

Makes 2 quarts
- 4 pounds fish heads (gills removed), skeleton, trimmings, etc.
- 1 large onion, quartered
- 2 stalks of celery, cut into 2" pieces
- 1 leek, sliced
- 1 small fennel bulb, quartered
- 2 bay leaves
- 8 sprigs Italian parsley
- 1 teaspoon black peppercorns
- 1/2 cup dry white wine
- 2 quarts cold water
- Salt, to taste (at the end of cooking)

Directions

Wash fish well to remove all blood. Place bones, onion, celery, leek, fennel, bay leaves, parsley, peppercorns, and white wine in a large stock pot and cover with cold water. Bring almost to a boil over high heat and immediately reduce to a low simmer for 30 minutes, uncovered. Periodically skim off any scum that rises to the top.

Strain stock through a fine-mesh strainer into a clean saucepan. Let cool and refrigerate overnight. The next day skim any congealed fat off the surface and place into airtight plastic pint containers. The stock should be very gelatinous. Freeze until needed. Stock can be stored in the freezer for up to four months.

Brodo Vegetale
Vegetable Stock

This is a recipe for a light vegetable stock. For a darker richer stock, place vegetables on a sheet pan covered with parchment paper, toss with 2-3 tablespoon of olive oil and a little salt. Roast in a pre-heated 400-degree Fahrenheit oven until browned. Be careful not to char the vegetables; otherwise your stock will taste bitter.

Makes 4 quarts

· 1 large yellow onion, peeled and quartered
· 1 leek, white part only cut in half lengthwise
  and then sliced into 2" pieces
· 2 stalks of celery, cut into 2" pieces
· 1 large carrot, cut into 2" pieces
· 2 bay leaves
· 8 sprigs Italian parsley
· 3-4 sprigs of thyme
· 1 teaspoon black peppercorns
· 4 quarts cold water
· Salt, to taste (at the end of cooking)

Directions

Place onion, leek, celery, carrot, bay leaves, parsley, thyme, and peppercorns in a large stock pot and cover with cold water. Bring almost a boil over high heat and immediately reduce to a low simmer for one hour, uncovered.

Strain stock through a fine-mesh strainer into a clean saucepan; add salt. Let cool and refrigerate or freeze. If you roasted the vegetables, there may be a little congealed fat on the surface that can easily be skimmed off. Place stock in airtight plastic pint containers. Stock can be stored in the freezer for up to four months.

Sources

D'Artagnan
(800) 327-8246
www.dartagnan.com
Fresh game and fowl, charcuterie,
foie gras, truffles, caviar.

Eataly Chicago
43 East Ohio Street
Chicago, IL 60611
(312) 521-8700
www.eataly.com
Wonderful selection of fresh fish and meats,
bottarga, cuttlefish ink, fresh and dried pasta,
truffles, cheeses, cured meat and sausages, olive
oil, fresh bread, wine and spirits.

Exotic Meat Market
(877) 398 0141
www.exoticmeatmarkets.com
Exotic meats and sausages from all over the
world, including suckling pig, suckling goat, and
wild hare.

Giannetti Artisans
(847) 926-0082
www.giannettiartisans.com
Artisan-made Italian specialty foods; vinegar,
olive oil, crackers, savory and sweet spreads and
sauces, honeys, dry porcini mushrooms, pista-
chio and chestnut flours, coffee and chocolate.

Janie's Mill
405 North 2nd Street
Ashkum, IL 60911
(815) 644-4032
www.themillatjaniesfarm.com
High quality, locally grown and milled certified
organic and whole kernel flours and grains.

King Arthur Flour
135 US Route 5 South
Norwich, VT 05055
(802) 649-3361
www.kingarthurflour.com
Excellent selection of flours, baking goods, SAF
Red instant yeast.

La Peonia Cose di Sardegna e Non Solo
Via delle Carrozze 85
00187 Roma, CA Italia
+39 06 679 8552
Whole and grated bottarga, Sardinian cheeses,
sausages, cuttlefish ink.

Marxfoods
(866) 588-6279
www.marxfoods.com
Wide variety of exotic meats, charcuterie, fowl,
fish and shellfish, caviar, roe, foie gras, truffles,
edible flowers.

Northwestern Cutlery
810 West Lake Street
Chicago, IL 60607
(888) 248-4449
www.nwcutlery.com
They call themselves the 'Candy Store for
Cooks' and they are. Large assortment of knives
and kitchen tools, (knife sharpening on site),
commercial cookware, chefs-wear, re-tinning
services .

Paulina Market
3501 North Lincoln Ave
Chicago, IL
(773) 248-6272
www.paulinamarket.com
A neighborhood butcher shop, sausage-maker,
smokehouse, and specialty grocery; fresh meats
and poultry; frozen selection of wild boar, rabbit,
duck, quail.

Publican Quality Meats
825 W. Fulton Market Street
Chicago, IL 60607
(312) 445-8977
www.publicanqualitymeats.com
A whole-animal butcher shop, specializing in
sausage and charcuterie; they also happen to
make some of the best bread in Chicago.

Savory Spice Shop
4753 North Lincoln
Chicago, IL 60625
(773) 293 4559
www.savoryspiceshop.com
Wide array of spices and herbs including
fennel pollen.

Glossary

Abbacchio alla romana
Braised lamb, Roman style.

Aglio
Garlic.

Agriturismo
A farmhouse converted to an inn and restaurant; generally, they produce what they serve.

Al dente
Pasta or rice that is slightly undercooked and firm to the bite.

Alimentari
Small grocery store.

Alla gricia
A typical Roman dish, pasta alla gricia is made with guanciale and Pecorino Romano.

Allo spiedo
Rotisserie or spit-roasted.

All'onda
Wavelike - the Venetians like their risotto all'onda.

Anatra in porchetta infinocchiata
Roast duck in the manner of porchetta.

Antipasto
Starter course.

Apericena
Aperitive accompanied by a large buffet.

Aperire
From the Latin verb "to open".

Aperitivo
Aperitive, before dinner drink.

Aperol
Italian bitter aperitive.

Arborio
An Italian short-grain rice, named after the town of Arborio in the Po Valley.

Bàcaro
Venetian wine bar that also serves cicchetti (bar food).

Baccalà
Salt cod.

Baccalà alla vicentina
Salt cod dish native to Vicenza, cooked with onions, milk, anchovies, and Parmigiano.

Baccalà fritto alla Romana
Salt cod, battered and fried.

Baccalà mantecato
Whipped salt cod.

Bigoli
Venetian whole wheat long pasta.

Biscotti
Italian cookies.

Bistecca alla fiorentina
Florentine T-bone steak.

Bombette di maiale
Stuffed pork rolls.

Bottarga
The salted and dried egg roe of either tuna or grey mullet.

Boule (Fr.)
Round loaf of rustic bread.

Branzino
Sea bass.

Bresaola
Cured beef.

Bruschetta
Toasted bread, often served with tomatoes and olive oil.

Bucatini
Long pasta with a hole running through it.

Bucatini all'amatriciana
Bucatini with guanciale (cured pork cheek) and tomatoes.

Buon appetito!
Enjoy your meal!

Burrata
Fresh Italian cow's milk cheese made from mozzarella and cream.

Cacciucco
Tuscan seafood stew with octopus, tomatoes, and red wine.

Caciocavallo
Stretched-curd cheese made from sheep's or cow's milk. Produced in Southern Italy, it is similar in taste to the aged Southern Italian provolone cheese.

Cacio e pepe
Pasta with cheese and black pepper.

Calamari
Squid.

Calvados (Fr.)
A variety of brandy made from apples in Normandy.

Cannellini
White beans (can substitute great northern or navy beans).

Cannoli
Sicilian shells of fried pastry, filled with sweet ricotta.

Cantucci
Tuscan almond cookies.

Capesante
Sea scallops.

Carciofi
Artichokes.

Cavolo nero
Black cabbage, Tuscan kale.

Charcuterie (Fr.)
Prepared and cured meat products such as sausages, hams, and pâtes.

Cicchetti
Venetian bar snacks.

Cime di Rapa
The tops of turnip greens, better known in the U.S. as broccoli rabe.

Cinghiale
Wild boar, often braised as a ragú.

Coda alla vaccinara
Oxtail stew in the manner of the butchers.

Coda di rospo
Monkfish tail.

Coniglio
Rabbit.

Contorno
Side dish.

Coppa, capocollo, capicola
Cured pork neck muscle.

Cornicione
The thick outer edge of a pizza.

Costolette di abbacchio
Baby lamb chops.

Cotechino
Gelatinous pork sausage in a natural casing.

Cotechino con lenticchie
Cotechino sausage with lentils; traditionally served on New Year's Eve.

Crostone di pane all'aglio
Toasted garlic bread.

Crostini
Toasted slices of bread.

Crudo
Raw seafood.

Cucina povera
Peasant cooking.

Digestivo
After dinner drink.

Dispensa
Pantry.

Doppio concentrato di pomodoro
Double-concentrated tomato paste.

Enoteca
Wine bar.

Erborinato
Blue cheese.

Fagiano
Pheasant.

Fagioli al fiasco
Beans cooked in a flask.

Glossary

Faraona
Guinea hen.

Fave
Broad beans.

Finocchio
Fennel.

Finocchiona
Fennel flavored Tuscan sausage.

Fiore sardo
A firm, sheep's milk cheese (pecorino) from Sardinia.

Fond (Fr.)
Concentrated brown bits of food that stick to the pan after browning meat and vegetables.

Formaggi misti
Mixed cheese plate or board.

Fornelli pronti
Butcher shops with attached kitchens.

Frittata
Italian omelet.

Frutti di mare
Seafood.

Fritto misto di mare
Mixed fried seafood.

Funghi
Mushrooms.

Funghi trifolati
Mushrooms sautéed in olive oil, garlic or shallots, and parsley.

Gaeta
Small brined black Italian olives (can substitute French niçoise olives).

Gamberi
Shrimp.

Gnocchi
Small, thick, and soft pasta dumplings made from semolina, or potatoes, flour, and eggs.

Gnummareddi
Liver, lungs and kidneys wrapped and cooked in lamb gut casings; often served on skewers.

Grano duro
Hard, high-protein wheat.

Guanciale
Cured pork cheeks, can substitute pancetta.

Guazzetto alla chioggiotta
Venetian fish stew enhanced with white wine vinegar.

Impepata di cozze
Peppered mussels.

In bianco
Without tomatoes.

Insalata
Salad.

Insalata di mare
Seafood salad.

La bella figura
"The beautiful figure" - it means to dress well; to make a good impression.

La dolce vita
The sweet life.

Lardo
Cured pork back fat.

Lardo di Colonnata
Cured pork back fat from the town of Colonnata.

Lardon (Fr.)
Small strip of guanciale or pancetta.

La vera cucina romana
Authentic Roman cuisine.

Lenticchie
Lentils.

Lepre
Hare.

Linguine
Long elliptical pasta, thicker than spaghetti.

Linguini alle vongole
Linguini with littleneck clams.

Lonza
Cured pork loin.

Malloreddus
Sardinian gnocchi made from semolina flour, water, and saffron.

Malloreddus alla campidanese
Sardinian gnocchi with sausage ragù.

Mercato
Market.

Misto mare affumicato
Mixed smoked seafood.

Mortadella
Large mild sausage made with emulsified meat.

Mostarda
Mustard with preserved fruits.

Napoletana
Naples style.

Negroni
Italian martini made with equal parts Campari, sweet vermouth, and gin.

Negroni sbagliato
Messed up Negroni, with gin replaced by Prosecco.

Nero di seppia
Black squid ink.

Orata
Seabream.

Orecchiette
Small handmade pasta in the shape of small ears from Puglia.

Paccheri
A type of short pasta in the shape of a large tube about 1 ½" long and 1" in diameter; mezzi paccheri is half-length paccheri.

Paccheri all'amatriciana di mare
Paccheri with guanciale, tomatoes, and seafood.

Paella (Sp.)
Spanish saffron-flavored rice dish made in a large flat pan.

Pancetta
Italian bacon, often rolled.

Pane carasau
Traditional flatbread from Sardinia.

Pangrattato
Breadcrumbs.

Panzanella
Tuscan bread and tomato salad.

Pappardelle
Large, wide, flat pasta noodles made with flour and eggs, originating from Tuscany.

Parmigiano
Hard granular cheese made from cow's milk.

Pasticceria
Italian pastry shop.

Pastis (Fr.)
Anise-flavoured apéritif from France.

Patate
Potatoes.

Patate al Forno
Roasted potatoes.

Patè di fegatini toscani
Chicken liver paté, Tuscan style.

Pecorino
Sheep's milk cheese.

Peperoncino
Small dried red peppers (red pepper flakes).

Pesto
A Ligurian sauce made with garlic, pine nuts, salt, basil leaves, grated Parmigiano or Pecorino sardo, and olive oil.

Piazza
Town square.

Piccione
Squab.

Pimentón (Sp.)
Smoky Spanish paprika, can be sweet, bitter or spicy.

Pizza Bianca
White pizza without tomatoes.

Pizzette
Tiny bite-size pizzas.

Planetaria
Stand mixer.

Glossary

Polenta
Italian cornmeal.

Pollame
Poultry.

Pollo alla cacciatora
Chicken hunter's style, made with onions and tomatoes.

Polpo alla griglia
Grilled octopus.

Pomodori di San Marzano
Heirloom plum tomatoes from the town of San Marzano sul Sarno near Naples. Grown in the volcanic soil created by Mount Vesuvius, their taste is more intense and sweeter than Roma tomatoes.

Porchetta
Spit-roasted whole suckling pig stuffed with its own liver, garlic, fennel, and rosemary.

Porcini
Popular brown-capped mushrooms; often added to braises to add earthy flavor.

Pranzo della domenica
Sunday lunch.

Primo
First course, usually pasta, soup, or rice.

Profumo
Scent.

Prosciutto
Cured ham.

Prosecco
Italian sparkling wine.

Puntarelle
Chicory.

Puntarelle alla romana
Chicory Roman style.

Puré di cavolfiore
Cauliflower purée.

Quaglie
Quail.

Ragù
Meat-based sauce often served with pasta.

Ribollita
Tuscan bread, bean, and cabbage soup.

Ricotta
Italian cheese made from milk whey left over from the production of other cheeses.

Rigatoni
A form of tube-shaped, slightly curved pasta about 2" long.

Rimacinata
Very fine, twice-milled flour.

Risotto
A northern Italian rice dish cooked with meat, fish, or vegetable broth until it reaches a creamy consistency.

Risotto ai frutti di mare, or **risotto alla pescatora**
Seafood risotto.

Risotto al nero di seppia
Risotto with cuttlefish ink.

Rombo
Turbot.

Rosticceria
A shop or informal restaurant specializing in roasted meats and fowl.

Rucola
Arugula.

Sagra
Festival.

Salmone affumicato
Smoked salmon.

Salumi
Cured meats and sausages.

Sardèle in saór
Sardines marinated in onions and white wine vinegar.

Sauté di calamari
Sautéed squid.

Sauté di spinaci
Sautéed spinach.

Scampi
Small edible lobster with a hard spiny shell
and long claws.

Scamorza affumicata
A dry, firm, smoked cheese from southern Italy
that's similar to low-moisture mozzarella.

Scottadito
Burned fingers.

Secondo
Main course, can be fish, or meat-based.

Semola
Finely ground durum flour.

Semolino
Semolina, coarsely ground durum flour.

Seppia
Cuttlefish.

Socarrat (Sp.)
The crispy rice on the bottom of the paella pan
after cooking.

Soffritto
Sautéed vegetables used a base for stock and
sauces; may contain onions, celery, carrots,
garlic and tomatoes.

Soppressata
Dried sausage found throughout Italy.

Sous-vide (Fr.)
A method of cooking food in plastic bag
submerged in a heated water bath.

Spaghetti al nero di seppia
Spaghetti with calamari and squid ink.

Spaghettoni
A long thick pasta, thicker than normal spaghetti.

Spaghettoni alla carbonara
Thick spaghetti with guanciale, egg yolks, cheese,
and black pepper.

Spaghettoni con le sarde
Thick spaghetti with sardines.

Speck
Speck hails from the South Tyrol region of
Northern Italy; it is a boned out ham, cured with
aromatic herbs and spices, smoked, and then
air-dried.

Spiaggia
Beach.

Stinco di agnello
Lamb shank.

Stracotto di manzo
Italian pot roast.

Tagliere
Wooden cutting board used to serve cured
meats and cheeses.

Tartufo
Truffle.

Tramezzini
White bread sandwiches with the crusts
removed.

Trofie
A short, thin, twisted pasta from Liguria.

Trofie al pesto con patate e fagioli
Trofie with pesto, potatoes, and green beans.

Utensili da Cucina
Kitchen equipment.

Vaporetto
Venetian public waterbus.

Vin Santo
Sweet dessert wine often served with cantucci
(Tuscan almond cookies).

Vitello tonnato
Veal with a tuna-caper sauce.

Zafferano
Saffron.

Zuppa
Soup.

Zuppa di pesce
Fisherman's stew.

Acknowledgments

Gregory Zychowicz, for inspiring this project and for his beautiful page layouts and book design.

Sister Marci Hermesdorf, for her patient and punctilious proofreading of my recipes and memoirs.

Mickey Sweeney, for suggesting the title of my book, and for drafting my biography.

Giacomo Polinelli, who carefully proofread my Italian.

Kaitlin Lucarelli, Eataly, Chicago, for her thoughtful wine pairings.

Amber Consolino, Eataly, Chicago, for her creative cheese selections.

Tonia Triggiano, with whom I have taught and worked with for many years on Dominican University's Summer Program in Florence.

Jean Bevier, who shares my love of a good Negroni and who co-directed Dominican University's Winter Interim Program in Rome for several years.

David Brody, for his generous foreword and shared passion for cooking.

Frank Spidale and Nancy Carey, for their support and enthusiasm for good food and community.

Dominican University, for supporting my passion for inspiring students to study abroad.

Undergraduate Research, Scholarship and Creative Investigations (URSCI), Dominican University, for the grant given to one of our Photography and Graphic Design Majors to prepare my images for printing.

Faculty Development Committee, Dominican University, for their generous grant supporting the publishing of this book.

Nicholas Lombardo, who helped prepare my iPhone photos for printing.

To all my guests, that have endured countless hours sitting on my uncomfortable Robert Mallet-Stevens dining chairs.

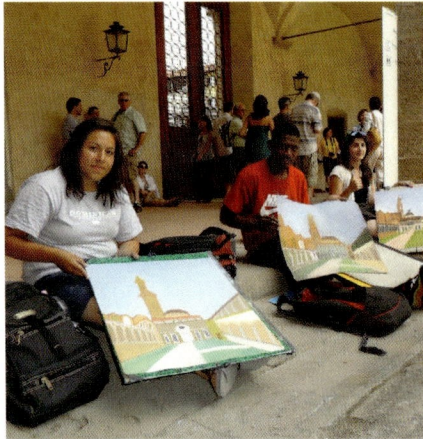

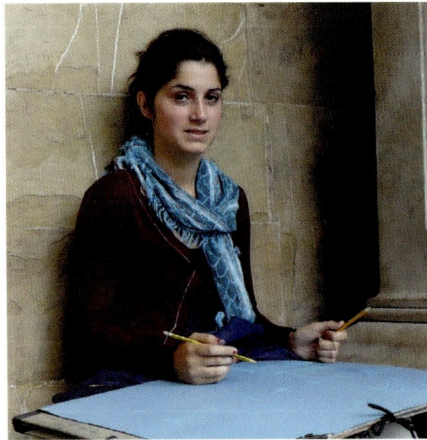

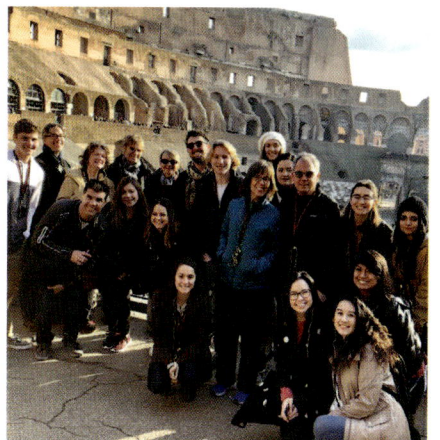

Index

Biography

Jeffery Cote de Luna's awakening to food as culture and cooking as community began when he, at age ten, moved with his parents to Madrid, Spain. This new European life was filled with fresh markets selling misshapen but delicious produce, local butchers selling spring lambs and suckling pigs, fish mongers selling baby eels and cuttlefish, and centuries-old Spanish restaurants and tapas bars located near the Plaza Mayor. The belief that sharing delicious meals should be a weekly, if not daily, occurrence, was encouraged by his Colombian mother, herself an excellent home cook.

In college, Jeffery spent a pivotal semester living with a large French family in the small town of Lisieux in Normandy. There, his appreciation of food as community was bolstered by weekend visits to the open-air market, where his host family knew each merchant by name. Together, he and the family would purchase the makings for homemade soups, buy fresh rabbits that would later be braised in red wine with prunes, buy some local cheese, and pick out crisp apples for rustic tarts. Fresh baguettes were delivered to the home every morning. Sunday meals would last an average of four to five hours and always ended with a glass or two of Calvados.

When he returned to the United States to pursue his Bachelor of Fine Arts at The School of the Art Institute of Chicago, Jeffery's love of detail, evident in his paintings and photographs, began to manifest itself in his burgeoning interest in cooking. After completing his Master of Fine Arts at Yale, Jeffery spent a decade traveling back and forth to Europe as well as to India, Nepal, Morocco and Egypt before he settled into teaching at Dominican University near Chicago. He has been the director of study abroad programs to Florence and Rome for the last twenty-five years. These experiences led to this book of recipes, musings, and memories.

Jeffery lives in Chicago and is an avid traveler, home cook, and all-season lakefront runner.